'Tarot Cards – The Hidden Symbols Explained'

Tarot Cards
The Hidden Symbols Explained

by

Derek Johnsen

Dedication

This book is dedicated to my long-suffering wife, Liz, who has had to put up with my studies, training and my absences when holding classes and teaching.

Also dedicated to my daughter, Claire, who has never lost faith in my work or in me.

Lastly, this book is dedicated to all the people that I have met throughout my development who have encouraged me to carry on with my work and for the support that Spirit itself has given to me over the years.

Love and Light.

Contents

Introduction

The Tarot cards are an enigma. To some people they are a simple fortune telling device, to others they are a window into the life and situation of the sitter, while yet others find them to be a bit scary, so something to be avoided. This is usually because of the utter nonsense portrayed in books, TV shows and films. All of this nonsense should be ignored, as Tarot Cards are perfectly safe to use. There are untrained people out there who try to use the Tarot, but because they are untrained, they might not give out the correct meanings or advice. This is not dangerous, just annoying.

As a psychic medium with nearly fifteen years' worth of experience at the time of writing, I find that the cards of the Tarot Deck are an invaluable tool when giving someone a reading. Apart from the actual spread of cards, each individual card is packed with hidden symbols that can help the reader gain a deeper insight into the life of the sitter. This is especially true if similar symbols appear in more than one card.

I have compiled my list of hidden symbols from the traditional Rider Waite deck and two other decks that are based on it. They are the Hanson Roberts deck and the 'Legacy of the Divine' deck by Ciro Marchetti. There are many different styles of Tarot Deck out there these days, but I prefer to stick with the more traditional styles based on the Rider Waite deck. This does not mean that the deck that you use and love should not be used, this is just my personal preference. You must always use the Tarot Deck that you feel drawn to.

This book is not a guide on how to use or read the Tarot Cards, as there are many books and websites out there that already cover this subject in depth. However, I would encourage all Tarot Card users to endeavour to compile their own list of interpretations for their own deck of cards and the symbols hidden within them. The reason for this is quite simple. As an example, think of a coin. For one person that coin might represent monetary gain for the sitter, while for another person it might indicate the need for the sitter to 'watch the pennies'. Each to their own, as whatever meaning you attach to a symbol is the correct meaning for you.

Every single Tarot Card is filled with hidden symbols, but some of the cards have more symbols than others. Some of the symbols appear within a card in one deck, but not in others. This is down to the artist behind the artwork. There is a possibility that the symbol that I attribute to a card does not appear in the same card of the deck that you own. Again, this is simply down to the artist, it does not mean that I have missed that symbol out, or that you are using the 'wrong' deck.

I have split these interpretations into two different formats for your convenience.

In Part One, you will find an alphabetical list of the most important hidden symbols to be found in the cards, as well as indicating which cards they can be found on.

In Part Two, you will find each card listed separately with a list of the hidden symbols to be found in that particular card. This gives you the choice of looking up a particular symbol to gain an understanding of its meaning, or to look up a particular card and read about all of the symbols to be found on that card.

I hope that this book will help you to develop a deeper understanding of your Tarot Cards, which will benefit both you and the sitter.

Love and Light.

Part One

Chapter One
A

Acorns
Symbolises life, fertility and regeneration.

Within a reading, an acorn can indicate that the sitter is undergoing a new phase in their life. They are possibly about to enter a new phase of personal growth. This could be within their personal or professional life. The acorn can represent the germination of a new idea that can only grow stronger.

Symbol found in some of these cards
The Four of Cups
The Ace of Coins

Airship
Symbolises flying. (Although only present in one card in one deck, I have included this symbol as it represents flying.)

Within a reading, an airship (or flying) indicates that the sitter needs to take a step back and look at their problems from another perspective. Only by changing their point of view will they be able to see a possible solution.

Symbol found in some of these cards
The Three of Wands

Altar
Symbolises a sacred place.

Within a reading, an altar implies that the sitter is in need of some personal space within their busy life. They need this personal space in order to have some time to themselves, maybe to pursue their interest in a hobby, or more importantly, to develop their individual spirituality.

Symbol found in some of these cards
The Devil
The King of Wands

Amethyst

Symbolises healing.

Within a reading, an amethyst (or the colour purple) tells the reader that the sitter is in need of some kind of healing. This could be the sitter's emotional issues or possibly their physical ailments. More simply, purple could suggest that the sitter needs some aspect of their life 'healed'.

Symbol found in some of these cards
The Ace of Swords

Angels

Symbolises divine messengers.

Within a reading, the appearance of an Angel in the spread represents that some kind of important information is coming the sitter's way. This could manifest itself in some sort of inspirational way, or even in a 'light bulb' moment. However the sitter receives this important information, they must not ignore it.

Symbol found in some of these cards
The Lovers
The Wheel of Fortune
Temperance
Judgement
The Queen of Swords

Angel Wings

Symbolises protection, affection, hope and happiness.

Within a reading, a pair of Angel wings on their own simply represents that some aspect of the sitter's life is going well. Even if they are unhappy with recent developments, they should be encouraged to concentrate on the good things that have happened and that are still going on around them.

Symbol found in some of these cards
The Lovers
The Chariot
The Wheel of Fortune
Temperance
Judgement

Ankh

Symbolises life. (The Ankh is an Egyptian symbol)

Within a reading, the appearance of the Ankh means that there is a good balance within the sitter's life at the moment. This could refer to a good balance in their relationship, their emotional state, their occupation or maybe even their finances.

Symbol found in some of these cards
The Emperor

Apple

Symbolises love, joy or knowledge.

Within a reading, the appearance of an apple suggests that the sitter is about to 'take a bite' out of that apple. This could represent the sitter is about to begin a new relationship, or that they are about to begin a new course of study.

Symbol found in some of these cards
The Lovers
The Three of Cups

Arch

Symbolises new beginnings.

Within a reading, the arch suggests that the sitter is about to take a new direction in life – whether they know it or not. A new opportunity is about to present itself to the sitter. This could be a new opening at work, a new career path for them to follow or possibly a new romantic involvement.

Symbol found in some of these cards
The Empress
The Chariot
Strength
The Four of Swords
The Six of Swords
The Page of Swords
The Queen of Swords
The Three of Coins
The Four of Coins
The Five of Coins
The Nine of Coins
The Ten of Coins
The Four of Wands
The Six of Wands

Arm Band
Symbolises belonging.
Within a reading, an armband represents the need of the sitter to belong to something. This might be a group or organisation that the sitter feels attracted to.
(An armband can be a piece of material, a piece of jewellery or even a tattoo.)

Symbol found in some of these cards
The Seven of Swords
The Queen of Cups
The Nine of Wands

Armour
Symbolises protection and strength.
Within a reading, the appearance of armour suggests that the sitter is feeling vulnerable in some way and that they feel the need to protect themselves from their perceived threat.

Symbol found in some of these cards
The Emperor
The Chariot
Death
The Four of Swords
The Five of Swords
The Knight of Swords
The Queen of Swords
The Knight of Cups
The Knight of Coins
The Knight of Wands

Axe Blades
Symbolises swift, but balanced justice.

Within a reading, axe blades suggest that the sitter is feeling inconvenienced or put out by recent events in their life. They are seeking a fast, but fair resolution to that problem.

Symbol found in some of these cards
The King of Swords

Chapter Two
B

Balcony
Symbolises an elevated position.

Within a reading, a balcony represents the sitter's need to raise themselves above it all and to look at things differently. This detached view of their life and/or problems will help them to see things more clearly.

Symbol found in some of these cards
The King of Coins

Banner (Flag)
Symbolises transformation.

Within a reading, a flag or banner is an announcement of change in the sitter's life and the flag is telling the world all about it. However, it can also represent a rallying call, asking people (probably family) to rally around the sitter's new cause.

Symbol found in some of these cards
Death
The Sun
Judgement

Baton
Symbolises spiritual authority or the development of ideas.

Within a reading, the baton represents the need of the sitter to take control of some aspect of the life, to be more authoritative in their dealings with others.

Symbol found in some of these cards
The Magician
The Chariot
The World

Battle

Symbolises conflict or struggle.

Within a reading, a battle scene represents that the sitter is experiencing some kind of struggle in their life. This could be an emotional struggle, or possibly a struggle with a legal procedure.

Symbol found in some of these cards

The Five of Swords
The Five of Wands
The Seven of Wands

Bed

Symbolises a retreat or a safe place.

Within a reading, a bed represents that the sitter might be feeling under pressure as a result of recent troubling events in their life. They need to sit down, relax and find some time for themselves away from the pressures of the day.

Symbol found in some of these cards

The Nine of Swords

Bee

Symbolises personal industry or hard work.

Within a reading, a bee represents that the sitter is leading an incredibly busy life. Probably juggling commitments with work, home, children and relationships. While the sitter might well thrive in this environment, it is wise to state the importance of taking time to relax as well.

Symbol found in some of these cards

The Ace of Coins

Begging Bowl

Symbolises the need of help from some quarter.

Within a reading, a begging bowl can represent the sitter needing and asking for help and assistance with some aspect of their life. By contrast, a begging bowl can also represent that the sitter is a generous giver of their time to help others.

Symbol found in some of these cards
The Five of Coins
The Six of Coins

Bench

Symbolises the need to study the details.

Within a reading, a bench represents the need for the sitter to take their time and to examine the details of the situation that they currently find themselves in. Symbolically 'laying out the plans' and studying them.

Symbol found in some of these cards
The Two of Swords
The Nine of Cups
The Three of Coins
The Eight of Coins

Bicycle (Bike)

Symbolises progress.

Within a reading, a bicycle represents the sitter's motivation and determination to proceed with their plans for the future. It is a symbol of progress and promising times ahead.

Symbol found in some of these cards
The Two of Coins

Bird

Symbolises rising above the normal.

Within a reading, a bird represents the sitter's need to lighten their thoughts. To rise above the problems of the material world and to look at the bigger picture. A bird can also symbolise the sitter's need to look at and to raise their individual spirituality.

Symbol found in some of these cards
The Wheel of Fortune
The Star
The World
The Seven of Swords
The Ace of Cups
The Three of Wands
The Four of Wands

Bird of Paradise

Symbolises the appreciation of beauty.

Within a reading, the bird of paradise represents the sitter's love and appreciation of all things beautiful. This could be art, nature or even surrounding themselves with beautiful objects, furniture or even clothes.

Symbol found in some of these cards
The Nine of Coins

Black Bird

Symbolises metaphorical death, as in something coming to an end.

Within a reading, the appearance of any species of black bird tells us that some aspect of the sitter's life is coming to an end. This could be a problem that they have been struggling with, or possibly a difficult phase in their life that they have been going through.

Symbol found in some of these cards
The Four of Swords

Blindfold

Symbolises our inability to see things clearly.

Within a reading, a blindfold represents the sitter's unwillingness to face the truth about some troubling aspect of their life. Basically that the sitter is turning a blind eye. It can also be a sign that something is being kept, or hidden from them.

Symbol found in some of these cards
The Two of Swords
The Eight of Swords

Blueprints

Symbolises the necessity of studying the details.

Within a reading, a blueprint represents that the sitter really needs to examine all of the details before committing themselves to some plan or relationship. It can also represent the fact that the sitter is going through some changes in their life.

Symbol found in some of these cards
The Eight of Coins

Boat (Ship)

Symbolises moving away from past events.

Within a reading, any boat or ship that appears in the spread represents moving on for the sitter. This could signify moving away from emotional troubles. It can also represent that the sitter has, or is about to move onto a new path, or different direction in life.

Symbol found in some of these cards
The Six of Swords
The King of Cups
The Two of Coins
The Three of Wands

Braids

Symbolises spiritual strength and health.

Within a reading, the appearance of braided hair (three strands of hair woven together) represents the sitter's mind, body and spirit being strengthened by a new influence in their life.

Symbol found in some of these cards
The Queen of Wands

Brick Wall

Symbolises a self-imposed barrier, or mental block.

Within a reading, a brick wall represents that the sitter is separating themselves from a problem, trying to shut that problem out of their mind. It is reluctance on the sitter's part to acknowledge what is happening around them. It can also represent the sitter holding themselves back or doubting themselves.

Symbol found in some of these cards
The Sun
The Five of Cups
The Six of Cups

Bridge

Symbolises dwelling on the past.

Within a reading, the appearance of a bridge represents the sitter's mind being stuck in past events. The bridge is a reminder to the sitter that it is time to move on to a new phase in their life.

Symbol found in some of these cards
The Five of Cups
The Four of Wands

Broken Glass

Symbolises that something is beyond repair.

Within a reading, the appearance of broken or shattered glass represents a final (and probably permanent) break in the sitter's life. This could be anything from the end of a relationship to the end of their current occupation.

Symbol found in some of these cards
The Five of Cups

Buckle (Silver)
Symbolises loyalty and trustworthiness.

Within a reading, a buckle can represent the sitter's need to 'buckle down' and get on with it. Whenever we use a buckle, we depend on it doing its job. In the same sense, a buckle can denote the sitter's sense of loyalty, trustworthiness and possibly even dependency.

Symbol found in some of these cards
The Five of Swords
The Four of Coins

Bull
Symbolises power and stability.

Within a reading, the appearance of a bull can represent quite a few things for the sitter. It could point to the sitter's resistance to change, as in being 'bull headed'. However, it can also suggest to the sitter that the time has come to stand their ground and fight for what they believe in.

Symbol found in some of these cards
The Wheel of Fortune
The World
The King of Coins

Butterfly
Symbolises transformation.

Within a reading, a butterfly suggests that it is time for the sitter to move away from their current phase in life to another, better phase. It can also represent that the sitter will have to change their way of thinking if they want to achieve their goals in life.

Symbol found in some of these cards
The Empress
The Queen of Swords
The King of Swords

Chapter Three
C

Caduceus
Symbolises balance, harmony, renewal and transformation.

Within a reading, a caduceus represents that the sitter is going through, or is about to go through a transitional stage in their life. Whatever this change may be, it will be beneficial to the sitter, bringing peace, balance and harmony into their life. Bodes well for new relationships.

Symbol found in some of these cards
The Two of Cups

Candelabra
Symbolises illuminating your way.

Within a reading, the appearance of a candelabra represents that the sitter needs to think carefully about which path in life they want to follow. Only by 'shining a light' on their chosen path will the sitter be able to navigate along that path, avoiding the obstacles.

Symbol found in some of these cards
The Six of Swords

Castle
Symbolises goals and achievements.

Within a reading, a castle represents the sitter's long and difficult journey to achieve their goal in life. This might be a long university degree course, or a long battle against illness. Whatever the sitter's goal is, they are well on their way to achieving it. On a simpler note, a castle can represent security or sanctuary.

Symbol found in some of these cards
The Chariot
The Eight of Swords

The Five of Cups
The Seven of Cups
The Ten of Cups
The Four of Coins
The Eight of Coins
The Nine of Coins
The Ten of Coins
The King of Coins
The Ace of Wands
The Four of Wands
The Ten of Wands

Cat

Symbolises spiritual ability.

Within a reading, the appearance of a cat in the spread denotes the sitter's quest for spiritual enlightenment. Not necessarily in a religious sense (although it could be), but possibly just seeking a path in life that can liberate them and make them feel free. In this case, a cat would indicate that the sitter is burdened with too many responsibilities.

Symbol found in some of these cards
The Ten of Cups
The Queen of Wands

Catacombs

Symbolises your deepest thoughts.

Within a reading, catacombs infer that the sitter is troubled with a series of unsettling thoughts from the darkest corners of their mind. However, it can also imply that the sitter is so lost in their deep thoughts that they are missing out on life.

Symbol found in some of these cards
The Six of Swords

Centaur

Symbolises unity of the mind and body.

Within a reading, the appearance of a centaur infers that the sitter might be in need of trying to strike a balance between their 'spiritual' and 'animal' sides. In other words, it is possible that they are knowingly doing something wrong and it is going against the grain.

Symbol found in some of these cards

The Eight of Wands

Chains

Symbolises restraint or restriction.

Within a reading, chains represent that the sitter is feeling held back, or being prevented from carrying out some action or other. If the chains are presented as some form of jewellery, then the sitter's problem is of a more delicate nature.

Symbol found in some of these cards

The Devil
The Two of Swords
The Six of Swords
The Nine of Cups
The Ten of Cups
The Six of Coins
The Ten of Coins
The Queen of Coins
The Six of Wands

Cherubs

Symbolises spiritual innocence.

Within a reading, a cherub can represent the sitter's innocence or naivety in the adult world. It could also represent that the sitter is one of life's gentler souls.

Symbol found in some of these cards
The Queen of Cups

Child/Children

Symbolises innocence and memories.

Within a reading, a child or children appearing in the spread signifies that the sitter might be living in the past too much. Childhood memories can be happy or sad, but should never be dwelled upon. However, children in the tarot can also represent promise for the future, or the beginning of a new venture, as well as a child-like enthusiasm for life.

Symbol found in some of these cards
The Sun
The Six of Cups
The Ten of Cups
The Six of Coins
The Ten of Coins

City / Village

Symbolises protection, harmony and teamwork.

Within a reading, a city, town or village appearing in the spread represents a place where people gather. Whatever the sitter is trying to do in life, they cannot do it alone. A group effort is required and the sitter should try and find the group that they need in order to accomplish their goals.

Symbol found in some of these cards
The Chariot
The Four of Coins
The Ten of Coins

Cliff Edge

Symbolises possible new opportunities.

Within a reading, a cliff edge can represent two things. The sitter is about to embark on a new path, which has been created by the arrival of a new opportunity in their life. On one hand, this is an exciting time for the sitter. On the other hand, they should take precautions, as there are potential pitfalls ahead.

<u>Symbol found in some of these cards</u>
The Fool
The Eight of Swords
The Five of Cups
The Three of Wands

<u>Clouds</u>
Symbolises transition.

Within a reading, clouds have different meanings depending on what colour they are. In the suit of Swords, most of the clouds are dark and fast moving, representing that the sitter is probably going through a troublesome (or stormy) period in their life. However, dark clouds like these can also represent confusion, or clouded judgement.

<u>Symbol found in some of these cards</u>
The Lovers
The Wheel of Fortune
The Tower
Judgement
The World
The Ace of Swords
The Three of Swords
The Five of Swords
The Page of Swords
The Knight of Swords
The Queen of Swords
The King of Swords
The Ace of Cups
The Four of Cups
The Seven of Cups
The Ace of Coins

The Ace of Wands
The Eight of Wands

Cobweb

Symbolises mystery, strength and growth.

Within a reading, the appearance of a cobweb represents that the choices that the sitter makes ultimately construct their life. We must 'weave' our lives as carefully and purposefully as the spider weaves his web.

Symbol found in some of these cards
Eight of Swords

Coconuts

Symbolises self-protection and self-projection.

Within a reading, a coconut represents that the sitter is displaying a tough 'outer shell', or public face to the world in an effort to protect themselves. They are however pretending that they are tougher than they really are. It will do the sitter no harm to allow their softer, inner self to made known to those around them.

Symbol found in some of these cards
The Nine of Cups

Coral

Symbolises abundance and prosperity.

Within a reading, the appearance of coral in the spread indicates that the sitter is enjoying the fruits of their labours. However, just like the coral itself, their current situation could be more fragile than they might realise. It is important that the sitter takes steps to protect themselves.

Symbol found in some of these cards
The Ace of Cups
The Knight of Cups

Corn

Symbolises fertility and rebirth.

Within a reading, sheaves of corn, or a whole cornfield, can represent that the sitter's mind is alive with ideas for their future. It is an exciting time for them as they plan out their new path in life. Corn can also represent fertility, pregnancy or childbirth.

Symbol found in some of these cards
The Empress

Crab

Symbolises perseverance and tenacity.

Within a reading, a crab can represent that the sitter might be clinging on to a hopeless or useless endeavour. They need to take a 'sideways' step and examine the situation in order to work out if the endeavour is worth the effort.

Symbol found in some of these cards
The Moon
The Two of Cups

Crossed Keys

Symbolises the opening of new doors.

Within a reading, crossed keys as shown on the Hierophant, represent the keys to heaven, as held by Saint Peter. However, within a tarot card spread, any key, however it is presented, represents the opening of a new door in the sitter's life.

Symbol found in some of these cards
The Hierophant

Crown

Symbolises authority and power.

Within a reading, the appearance of a crown can signify many things. It could suggest that the sitter needs authority in their life. Possibly that the sitter desires recognition for their achievements. Or even that the sitter desires more control of their life, which might feel a little out of control to them at the moment.

Symbol found in some of these cards
The Empress
The Emperor
The Hierophant
Justice
Death
The Tower
The Ace of Swords
The Queen of Swords
The King of Swords
The Seven of Cups
The Queen of Cups
The King of Cups
The Four of Coins
The Queen of Coins
The King of Coins
The Queen of Wands
The King of Wands

Crutch
Symbolises physical and spiritual support.

Within a reading, the appearance of a crutch represents the fact that the sitter is in need of some kind of support. As a rule, this is more likely to be some kind of emotional support. However, it can also represent the sitter's need for financial support, or support from colleagues at work.

Symbol found in some of these cards
The Five of Coins

Crystal Ball or Glass Globe

Symbolises enlightenment.

Within a reading, a crystal ball or glass globe implies that the sitter is in need for clarity and focus in their life. Some aspect of their life is causing them great confusion. They need to know what it is that they want (or do not want) in life. Once they have figured this out, their path ahead will become clearer.

Symbol found in some of these cards

The Emperor

Chapter Four
D

Dark Skies (Storm Clouds)
Symbolises potential troubles.

Within a reading, the appearance of dark skies, or storm clouds, represents that the sitter is probably going through a rough patch in their life. On the other hand, dark skies, or stormy looking clouds, can also represent confusion about some issue in the sitter's life, or possibly that they are experiencing clouded judgement.

Symbol found in some of these cards
The Ace of Swords
The Three of Swords
The Five of Swords
The Page of Swords
The Knight of Swords
The Queen of Swords
The King of Swords

Devil
Symbolises materialism.

Within a reading, the appearance of the Devil represents that the sitter is probably more concerned with the material world and all of the pleasures that it can bring. It is really time for the sitter to start looking beyond the material world and look within themselves to discover what is really important in life.

Symbol found in some of these cards
The Devil

Dog/Dogs
Symbolises loyalty or devotion.

Within a reading, whenever a dog (or dogs) appear in the spread it represents that the sitter might be experiencing loyalty issues. However, a dog can also represent that the sitter is on the right track in life, as dogs are symbolic of stability and steadfastness.

Symbol found in some of these cards
The Fool
The Moon
The Ten of Cups
The Ten of Coins

Dolphin
Symbolises friends, happiness and amusement.

Within a reading, the appearance of a dolphin represents that the sitter is enjoying a good social life at the moment. It can also represent that the sitter is exploring and enjoying the playful side of their nature.

Symbol found in some of these cards
The King of Cups

Door (Portal)
Symbolises the opening to a new path in life.

Within a reading, any door of any shape, size or colour represents that the sitter is about to open that door and start out on a new path in life. Of course, this door may well have just opened for the sitter and they have already begun their journey.

Symbol found in some of these cards
The Four of Coins
The Five of Coins
The Seven of Wands

Dove
Symbolises peace, purity and love.

Within a reading, a dove can represent many things. It is a symbol of peace and love, but it is also regarded by many as a true spiritual sign. If the sitter has been experiencing a troubling time recently, the dove can be regarded as a sign that their troubles will soon be over and that peace and tranquillity will soon be restored.

Symbol found in some of these cards
The Star
The Ace of Cups

Dragon
Symbolises wisdom, strength and courage.

Within a reading, the appearance of a dragon in the spread represents that the sitter needs to rise over their present circumstances in order to see things more clearly. Whatever their currant problem is, they need moral strength and personal courage to overcome it.

Symbol found in some of these cards
The Seven of Cups
The Ace of Wands
The Five of Wands
The Six of Wands
The Page of Wands
The Knight of Wands
The King of Wands

Chapter Five
E

Eagle

Symbolises a connection to spiritual powers, Spirit Guides and Teachers.

Within a reading, the appearance of an eagle is a really good sign for any sitter who is trying to develop their psychic ability. It represents the fact that the sitter is doing well in their studies and that they will soon rise to the elevated heights that they are trying to achieve.

Symbol found in some of these cards
The Emperor
The Wheel of Fortune
The World
The Ace of Swords
The Knight of Swords
The King of Swords

Earth (The Planet)

Symbolises Nature (as in Mother Earth) fertility and life.

Within a reading, the appearance of planet Earth indicates that the sitter has a keen affinity with nature and the natural world. As the Earth is a sphere, this can also indicate that the sitter is currently experiencing completeness in some aspect of their life.

Symbol found in some of these cards
The Fool
The World

Chapter Six
F

Fairy

Symbolises paranormal powers and imagination.

Within a reading, the appearance of a fairy in the spread indicates that the sitter probably possesses psychic abilities, whether they are aware of it or not. The images that flash through their minds are being wrongly dismissed as simple imagination.

Symbol found in some of these cards
The Seven of Cups

Falling Man

Symbolises a fall from grace.

Within a reading, the image of the falling man indicates that the sitter is feeling in a precarious position at present. Whether relating to a relationship or work situation, the sitter feels that they are walking a tightrope and could slip at any moment.

Symbol found in some of these cards
The Tower

Fan

Symbolises stepping back and assessing the situation.

Within a reading, a fan represents that the sitter is more than likely feeling overwhelmed by their current situation. It is time for the sitter to 'cool it'. They need to take a break and assess their position before carrying on.

Symbol found in some of these cards
The Queen of Swords

Feathers

Symbolises spiritual evolution.

Within a reading, a feather (or feathers) represents that the sitter is becoming aware of their spiritual side and that they are probably keen to advance that interest. Within the spiritual movement, feathers are universally recognised as a sign from Spirit, or a loved one that has passed.

Symbol found in some of these cards
The Page of Swords
The Page of Cups
The Six of Coins
The Knight of Wands

Female Symbol
Symbolises femininity.

Within a reading, the female sign obviously relates to femininity. However, if the sitter is a male, he should try and get in touch with his feminine side.

Symbol found in some of these cards
The Two of Cups

Ferryman
Symbolises transition.

Within a reading, rivers or the Ferryman indicates that the sitter is at a threshold in life. It represents a crossing over from one path in life to another. However, some believe that the Ferryman can symbolise the presence of spirit guides or guardians.

Symbol found in some of these cards
The Six of Swords

Fire (Flames)
Symbolises transformation.

Within a reading, fire or flames represents that the sitter is going through some kind of transition in their life. They can also represent that the sitter might need to make some kind of change, alteration or modification to their lifestyle.

Symbol found in some of these cards
Temperance
The Devil
The Tower
The Five of Swords
The Ten of Cups
The Ace of Wands
The Knight of Wands
The King of Wands

Fish
Symbolises intuition and creativity.

Within a reading, fish have many meanings. Fish can represent knowledge, inspiration or the mental balancing of the sitter's thoughts. The sitter might be a very creative person, or might possess a high level of intuition or spiritual ability. On the other hand, it could represent the fact that the sitter is involved with, or is dealing with a 'slippery' person or situation.

Symbol found in some of these cards
The Ace of Cups
The Page of Cups
The Knight of Cups
The Queen of Cups

Flag
See banner.

Flagstones
Symbolises a solid base or foundations.

Within a reading, flagstones can represent the sitter's need, or possibly their search for stability in life. This could manifest itself as the sitter's search for a job, somewhere to live or a stable relationship.

Symbol found in some of these cards
The Four of Coins

Fleur-de-lis
Symbolises adaptability.

Within a reading, some believe that the three shoots of the fleur-de-lis (a stylised lily) represent the Father, the Son and the Holy Spirit. Others prefer the representation of the unity of mind, body and spirit. Whichever representation you are drawn to, the three spreading shoots of the fleur-de-lis refer to the sitter’s ability to adapt to changing circumstances.

Symbol found in some of these cards
The Knight of Swords

Flowers
Symbolises new life and regeneration.

Within a reading, different individual flowers have different meanings. However, flowers in general represent that the sitter is opening (or has already opened) themselves up to new ideas, beliefs or experiences, all of which they will benefit from.

Symbol found in some of these cards
The Empress
The Three of Cups
The Six of Cups
The Ten of Cups
The Ace of Coins
The Nine of Coins
The Page of Coins
The Queen of Coins
The Two of Wands
The Four of Wands

Fruit

Symbolises good health and love.

Within a reading, any fruit can represent that the sitter has started out on a new path in life. All fruits have seeds and those seeds, when plated, will grow. (The 'seed' of a new idea for example.) so any fruit represents growth and new beginnings for the sitter. Also, as a symbol of fertility, fruit can represent pregnancy.

Symbol found in some of these cards
The Nine of Cups

Fur

Symbolises affluence, status and luxury.

Within a reading, animal fur depicts the sitter's desire for status, wealth and good fortune in life. However, in order to achieve those goals, the sitter will have to make some sacrifices.

Symbol found in some of these cards
The Page of Swords
The King of Swords
The Knight of Coins
The King of Coins

Chapter Seven
G

Gauntlets (Gloves)

Symbolises a challenge.

Within a reading, the appearance of a gauntlet represents that the sitter is facing some kind of challenge in their life, as in 'throwing down the gauntlet'. This could be a challenge that they face, or a challenge that they have made.

Symbol found in some of these cards
The Five of Swords
The Seven of Swords
The Knight of Swords
The Five of Wands
The Six of Wands
The Nine of Wands

Ghostly Hands

Symbolises troubling thoughts.

Within a reading, the image of ghostly hands does not appear very often, but when it does it indicates that the sitter is being plagued with disturbing thoughts or unpleasant dreams. This is having a serious affect on the sitter, so they must get to the root of the problem that is causing these troubling thoughts or dreams and try to sort them out.

Symbol found in some of these cards
The Nine of Swords

Globe

Symbolises achievement.

Within a reading, globes are sometimes shown as crystal balls or as the world, both of which are round in shape. Any round object or circle represents completion. This refers to the fact that the sitter is about to achieve some goal in their life. It is a sign of completion and infers that the sitter has the 'world at their fingertips'.

Symbol found in some of these cards
The Emperor
The Two of Wands

Goblet/Chalice
Symbolises family and tradition.

Within a reading, the appearance of a goblet or chalice indicates that family is extremely important to the sitter. It implies that the sitter probably possesses a pretty traditional view of what family life means to them. In particular, children and grandchildren mean everything to them and are their very reason for being.

Symbol found in some of these cards
Temperance
All of the Cups cards.

Gold Chain of Office
Symbolises position and authority.

Within a reading, a gold chain of office (as opposed to a gold necklace) implies that the sitter is chasing after, or has recently achieved a long sought after role in life. This could be a promotion at their present place of employment, or possibly a new job that they have recently started.

Symbol found in some of these cards
The Nine of Cups

Grapes (Grapevines)
Symbolises bountifulness.

Within a reading, grapes or grapevines imply that the sitter is a very hospitable and generous person, who enjoys sharing the fruits of their bounty (work or good fortune) with others. Can also signify abundance and fertility within the sitter's life.

Symbol found in some of these cards

The Seven of Pentacles
The Nine of Pentacles
The Ten of Pentacles
The King of Pentacles
The Three of Cups
The Four of Wands

Chapter Eight
H

Hammer

Symbolises getting a job done.

Within a reading, the appearance of a hammer refers to the fact that the sitter is trying to get a point across, or that the sitter is trying to get a job done, but trying to ensure that it is done properly. It can also suggest that the sitter needs to 'hammer out' the details regarding their work or a project that they are involved in.

Symbol found in some of these cards
The Three of Coins
The Eight of Coins

Hand

Symbolises transmission or give and take.

Within a reading, a hand or a pair of hands on their own implies that the sitter should understand that the problem that they are dealing with at this moment in their life, can only be solved with some kind of compromise. Hands give and receive, or give and take, so should the sitter.

Symbol found in some of these cards
The Ace of Coins
The Ace of Wands
The Ace of Swords
The Ace of Cups

Hawks

Symbolises freedom and growth.

Within a reading, the appearance of a hawk within a spread suggests that it is time for the sitter to free their minds from cluttered thoughts. It can also suggest that this is a time in the sitters life when they need to focus on what is ahead, as they might have to prepare for a future role of responsibility.

Symbol found in some of these cards
The Knight of Swords

Heart
Symbolises love, joy and affection.

Within a reading, a heart suggests that the sitter needs to pay attention to the things that are important to them. The heart is also a symbol of truth, courage and loyalty. In that respect, it is probably time for the sitter to take stock of other people in their life, in order to see if these issues are reciprocated.

Symbol found in some of these cards
The Lovers
The Three of Swords

Hedgehog
Symbolises rebirth.

Within a reading, because the hedgehog hibernates during the winter and re-emerges in the spring, it is universally regarded as a symbol of rebirth or renewal. For the sitter, this represents a new and busy phase in their life, possibly the awakening of a talent that the sitter was unaware that they had.

Symbol found in some of these cards
The Ace of Coins

Helmet
Symbolises protection.

Within a reading, a helmet can suggest that the sitter is feeling vulnerable in some way and is looking for a way to protect themselves from the cause. Usually a helmet has a plume or crest on top of it for identification. This could suggest that the sitter is searching for acceptance in some way.

Symbol found in some of these cards
Justice
The Knight of Cups
The Knight of Coins
The Six of Wands
The Knight of Wands

Hills
Symbolises obstacles.

Within a reading, the appearance of hills in the spread suggests that the sitter is facing obstacles in their life that they need to overcome. However daunting or impossible these hurdles might appear to be for the sitter, they need to remove these obstacles in their life in order to move on.

Symbol found in some of these cards
Temperance
Judgement
The Two of Cups
The Page of Coins
The Nine of Wands

Hoe
Symbolises resourcefulness.

Within a reading, the hoe (or any other tool) suggests that the sitter can make their present path a lot easier to negotiate if they use the resources (the tools) that they have available to them. In other words, should the sitter carry on doing things the hard way, or is it time to ask for some help?

Symbol found in some of these cards
The Seven of Coins

Hood
Symbolises protection.

Within a reading, a hood represents that the sitter feels the need to protect themselves from someone or something. It can also suggest that the sitter is trying to hide something from someone, or possibly that someone is trying to hide something from the sitter. Lastly, it can imply that the sitter really needs to shut themselves away from others for a while, just to have some alone time.

Symbol found in some of these cards
The Hermit

Horns
Symbolises physical prowess.

Within a reading, the appearance of horns indicates that the sitter is experiencing (or is in need of) fighting spirit in order to overcome a challenge that they are currently facing. It can also infer that the sitter has to take this challenge head on (by the horns), as there is really no other way of dealing with it.

Symbol found in some of these cards
The Devil
The Knight of Coins
The Knight of Wands
The King of Wands

Horse
Symbolises strength and freedom.

Within a reading, a horse refers to the sitter's personal drive and a desire to free themselves from the current path that they are following. The sitter has the strength and stamina to easily achieve this goal, but they have to believe in themselves. Horses are also regarded as a deep spiritual sign, which might hint at the sitter's need for some spiritual guidance. Maybe the sitter needs to free themselves from old beliefs.

Symbol found in some of these cards
The Chariot
Death
The Sun
The Knight of Swords
The Knight of Cups
The Knight of Coins
The Six of Wands
The Knight of Wands

Hourglass

Symbolises the passage of time.

Within a reading, the appearance of an hourglass refers to the fact that the sitter is running out of time. The sitter has something that is blocking their progress and they must deal with it as soon as possible. They need to do what needs to be done in order to get on with their life.

Symbol found in some of these cards
The Hanged Man
The Devil
The World

House (Cottage)

Symbolises safety and security.

Within a reading, houses or cottages usually appear in the background of the card. This implies that for the sitter (as for all of us) their home is always in the back of their mind. Our homes are our places of sanctuary in our increasingly fast-paced and busy lives. For the sitter, home is where the heart is and they probably wish that they could spend more time there, implying that maybe they are working too hard and too many long hours.

<u>Symbol found in some of these cards</u>

The Six of Cups

The Ten of Cups

Chapter Nine
I, J & K

Ice

Symbolises difficult territory.

Within a reading, ice usually appears on mountaintops in the background of a card. This suggests that the sitter knows within themselves (at the back of their minds) that they need to calm down (cool it) and react less to a negative situation that they are facing.

Symbol found in some of these cards
The Fool
The Hermit
The Tower
Judgement

Infinity Symbol

Symbolises endless possibilities.

Within a reading, the Infinity Symbol (The Lemniscate) represents the never-ending possibilities in our lives. For the sitter, it implies that they possess the necessary endless energy to face whatever life throws at them. It can also represent everlasting love.

Symbol found in some of these cards
The Magician
Strength
The World
The King of Swords
The Two of Coins

Jewellery

Symbolises financial security.

Within a reading, the appearance of jewellery can suggest that the sitter has a desire, or a need for financial security. It can also represent the sitter's aspirations for wealth. The sitter probably has a plan forming in their mind regarding how they can improve their financial status.

Symbol found in some of these cards
The Seven of Cups

Key
Symbolises unlocking potential.

Within a reading, a key usually represents the fact that the sitter is about to unlock a hidden talent, or that they are about to open a new door (new path) in their life. Depending on the sitter's circumstances, a key can also represent closing a door on some part of their life, as in something coming to an end for the sitter.

Symbol found in some of these cards
The Hierophant
The Ten of Coins
The Two of Wands

Kite
Symbolises aspirations.

Within a reading, a kite can represent the sitter's hopes, dreams and aspirations. However, it ca also represent the sitter's desire to escape their responsibilities.

Symbol found in some of these cards
The Six of Cups

Chapter Ten
L

Ladybird (Ladybug)

Symbolises good fortune

Within a reading, the appearance of a ladybird recommends that the sitter should try to stop their negative thoughts and concentrate on the things that fill their heart with joy. Also, the ladybird is a symbol of good luck, so possibly the sitter's future might take a turn for the better.

Symbol found in some of these cards

The Ace of Coins

Lantern (Lamp)

Symbolises finding your way.

Within a reading, a lantern (or lamp) indicates that the sitter might be struggling with life at the moment and could be feeling confused about their circumstances. Mentally, the sitter needs to use the lantern to light their way and find their true path in life.

Symbol found in some of these cards

The Hermit

Laurel Wreath

Symbolises achievement.

Within a reading, the appearance of a laurel wreath indicates that the sitter has recently achieved something in their life that they are very proud of. This could be anything from passing an exam, getting the job that they have always wanted or overcoming some personal problem that has been holding them back.

Symbol found in some of these cards

The World
The Ace of Swords
The Seven of Cups
The Six of Wands

Leopard

Symbolises strength.

Within a reading, the leopard infers that the sitter needs to start trusting their inner self a lot more, as they possess a strength of character that they seem to be unaware of. A leopard can also represent a period of renewal for the sitter, as in 'changing your spots'. It is during this period of renewal that the sitter will need to draw on their inner strength to see it through to its successful end.

Symbol found in some of these cards

The Empress

Library

Symbolises knowledge.

Within a reading, the appearance of a library, or a collection of books, relates to the gathering together of knowledge and/or wisdom. For the sitter, books can indicate a period of study that they are going through or that they are about to begin. This study and gathering of knowledge bodes well for the sitter, as it will open new doors for them.

Symbol found in some of these cards

The Magician

Lightening

Symbolises a destructive force.

Within a reading, lightening suggests that the sitter must start to pay attention to their surroundings. It indicates that there is a destructive or disruptive force at work in their life. The sitter must identify that force (or indeed the person behind it) and stop it before it causes any more damage.

Symbol found in some of these cards

The Tower

Lilies

Symbolises purity, love and relationships.

Within a reading, the appearance of a lily, or lilies, refers to a period of personal growth and development for the sitter. The lily can also indicate that the sitter (or someone that they are close to) is about to embark on a new relationship or that there is a birth in their immediate future.

Symbol found in some of these cards
The Magician
Temperance
The Ace of Coins
The Ace of Wands

Lion

Symbolises courage and strength.

Within a reading, a lion can indicate that the sitter has the necessary personal courage and emotional strength required to overcome the difficulties that they are facing right now. Just as the lion is fearless, it is time for the sitter to conquer his or her own fears. Fear can hold us back, so conquering your fears will is the key to the sitter achieving the success that they desire.

Symbol found in some of these cards
Strength
The Wheel of Fortune
The World
The Two of Cups
The Queen of Wands
The King of Wands

Lizard

Symbolises renewal and rebirth.

Within a reading, the appearance of a lizard infers that the sitter is about to enter a phase of clear vision and enlightenment in their life. This is most probably connected to the sitter's realisation that a new opportunity is presenting itself to them. This new opportunity will offer the sitter a whole new start.

<u>Symbol found in some of these cards</u>
The Page of Wands
The Knight of Wands
The King of Wands

<u>Lobster</u>
Symbolises hidden psychic ability.

Within a reading, a lobster (or a crab or crayfish) is a reminder to the sitter that they should try and lose their hard outer protective shell and allow their visionary inner self to come out and develop. Those 'gut feelings' that the sitter is experiencing are actually a strong psychic talent that they possess and that it is time to set it free.

<u>Symbol found in some of these cards</u>
The Moon

Chapter Eleven
M

Magpie

Symbolises balance in life.

Within a reading, a magpie can refer to the sitter's tendency to chase after false ideas or perceptions. Its appearance in the spread is a reminder to the sitter that the time has come to re-evaluate their priorities. The magpie's love of shiny or glittery things can suggest that the sitter could be more interested in the material side of life and ignoring their spiritual side.

Symbol found in some of these cards
The Seven of Swords

Manta Rays

Symbolises grace and flow.

Within a reading, the appearance of a manta ray is quite rare, but it represents grace, flow and wisdom. As manta rays are sensitive to the flows of the ocean's energy, it is a reminder to the sitter that they should start to tune into the flow of their own spiritual energy.

Symbol found in some of these cards
The Knight of Cups

Moat

Symbolises protection.

Within a reading, a moat suggests that the sitter is feeling vulnerable at the moment. The sitter feels in need of protecting themselves in some aspect of their life, which is probably an emotional issue. A moat can also represent the sitter's need to cut themselves off from something, to stop it in its tracks, possibly the emotional issue mentioned above.

Symbol found in some of these cards
The Four of Wands

Moon

Symbolises cycles.

Within a reading, the appearance of the moon in a spread indicates that the sitter is moving from one phase of their life to another. Whatever transition is taking place in the sitter's life, it is for the sitter's overall good and/or wellbeing. The moon can also indicate that the sitter is quite a spiritual person, who might very well be starting to realise that they have psychic abilities themselves.

Symbol found in some of these cards

The High Priestess
The Chariot
The Hanged Man
The Tower
The Moon
The Two of Swords
The Seven of Swords
The Eight of Cups
The Nine of Wands

Mountains

Symbolises challenges.

Within a reading, mountains usually appear in the background of the card. For the sitter, this suggests that they are facing seemingly insurmountable challenges, but that the sitter is trying to ignore them, pushing them to the back of their mind. If mountains appear in the majority of the spread, this indicates that the time has come for the sitter to face those challenges and to deal with them.

Symbol found in some of these cards

The Fool
The Emperor
The Lovers
Strength

The Hermit
The Wheel of Fortune
Judgement
The Six of Swords
The Ten of Swords
The Page of Swords
The Knight of Swords
The Eight of Cups
The Knight of Cups
The Page of Coins
The Queen of Coins
The Ace of Wands
The Two of Wands
The Seven of Wands
The Eight of Wands
The Ten of Wands
The Page of Wands
The Knight of Wands
The Queen of Wands
The King of Wands

Mouse

Symbolises scrutiny.

Within a reading, a mouse represents examination. As mice are pretty short-sighted, they have to examine their surroundings with great care. For the sitter, this suggests that they must pay attention to detail. If they are faced with legal documents or a contract for example, they must scrutinise that document and examine every detail before they sign it. Failure to do so could result in future problems.

Symbol found in some of these cards
The Empress

Chapter Twelve
N & O

Nautilus Shells

Symbolises renewal.

Within a reading, it should be understood that the nautilus shell grows throughout its life, constantly adding new and larger chambers as it grows. For the sitter, this is a symbol that represents a period of expansion and renewal in some aspect of their life.

Symbol found in some of these cards
The King of Cups

Nuts

Symbolises toughness.

Within a reading, the appearance of any kind of nut usually represents toughness due to their hard outer shell. For the sitter however, this can symbolise that the time has come for them to toughen up in some way. It might be difficult for them to change their basic nature in this way, but it must be done if they wish to succeed with their present plans.

Symbol found in some of these cards
The Nine of Cups

Octopus

Symbolises flexibility.

Within a reading, an octopus has nearly as many meanings as the octopus has tentacles. It can represent flexibility, unpredictability or even creativity. However, as far as the sitter is concerned, it is probably a warning to cut back on their workload and responsibilities, as they have their fingers in too many pies and the strain is starting to tell on them.

Symbol found in some of these cards
The Seven of Cups
The Eight of Cups

Orrery (model of the solar system)
Symbolises personal viewpoint.

Within a reading, the Orrery suggests that the sitter likes to be the centre of attention. However, this character trait can sometimes be misinterpreted as being a bit needy, so the sitter needs to be made aware of this fact. By contrast, it can also represent that the sitter enjoys being at the centre of things – in the thick of it.

Symbol found in some of these cards
The Sun

Owl
Symbolises wisdom.

Within a reading, an owl can be interpreted in two ways. It can represent the fact that the sitter needs to 'wisen up' to the circumstances that presently surround them. However, it can also mean that the sitter already possesses the required wisdom to deal with whatever they have been confronted with recently. The surrounding cards will indicate which interpretation applies.

Symbol found in some of these cards
The High Priestess

Chapter Thirteen
P

Paddle
Symbolises independence.

Within a reading, the appearance of a paddle is an indication to the sitter that the time has come to 'paddle your own canoe'. In other words, the time has come for the sitter to start acting independently and work towards deciding their own fate. The time has come to stop relying on, or listening to others.

Symbol found in some of these cards
The Six of Swords

Path (Road)
Symbolises life choices.

Within a reading, a path or a road refers to the fact that the sitter is facing a new path in life. The sitter might be about to set out on that new path, or may already have taken their first few steps on it. Either way, this path represents a whole new and potentially exciting future for the sitter. If they are having any doubts about this new path, they shouldn't worry, as it will be the right choice for them.

Symbol found in some of these cards
Temperance
The Moon
The Ten of Swords
The Ace of Coins
The Knight of Coins
The Ten of Wands

Pearls
Symbolises wisdom.

Within a reading, pearls are said to represent wisdom that has been acquired through experience. As far as the sitter is concerned, pearls infer that he or she has learned a life lesson recently, having gone through an experience that was probably an unpleasant one. As the saying goes, 'wise after the event'. However, this newly gained wisdom will prepare them for similar future events and allow them to handle it better.

Symbol found in some of these cards
The Two of Cups
The Queen of Cups

Pentangle
Symbolises the five senses

Within a reading, the Devil card represents materialism. The appearance of a pentangle on this card can indicate that the sitter is too concerned with the materialistic side of life and not paying enough attention to their spiritual self. The pentangle can also represent the five virtues, which are generosity, fellowship, chastity, courtesy and charity. The sitter should consider trying to follow one of these paths to start their journey away from materialism.

Symbol found in some of these cards
The Devil

Pillar
Symbolises stability.

Within a reading, a pillar or pillars, represent strength, stability and balance. A single pillar can suggest that the sitter is the one who is supporting those around them, as in 'a pillar of strength'. When two pillars appear, usually at each side of the card, this could indicate that the sitter should consider their problems in a more diplomatic, or balanced way. Rather than left or right or black and white, the sitter should try to consider a more central view. In other words, the sitter should adopt a new perspective, a middle-of-the-road approach when tackling their problems.

Symbol found in some of these cards
The High Priestess
The Emperor
The Hierophant
The Lovers
Strength
Justice
The Hanged Man
Death
The Devil
The Moon
The Four of Swords
The Nine of Swords
The King of Swords
The King of Cups
The Three of Coins
The King of Coins
The King of Wands

Pitcher
Symbolises what lies within.

Within a reading, a pitcher (or jug) is a vessel or a container. What is of interest to us, is what is in the pitcher. It is exactly the same principle for the sitter. The sitter needs to re-examine themselves and decide what kind of vessel are they? What type of contents fill their heart or soul? It should be pure, but if it is not – then why not? Is there anything that they can do to improve their spiritual core?

Symbol found in some of these cards
The Star

Ploughed Fields

Symbolises care and planning.

Within a reading, ploughed fields remind the sitter that 'we reap what we sew'. The sitter must keep in mind that whatever they do today will ultimately affect their future plans and outcomes. The sitter will benefit from a bit of careful thought and planning before they start any new venture. It would be helpful if the sitter remembers that ploughed fields can also represent time. Just as it takes time for crops to grow, so it takes time for our plans to come to fruition, so the sitter must try and understand that patience will be required.

Symbol found in some of these cards

Page of Coins
Knight of Coins
The Ten of Wands

Pomegranate

Symbolises femininity.

Within a reading, the pomegranate is a symbol in many cultures that represents love, marriage and fertility. A pomegranate could infer that the sitter is thinking about starting a family, or possibly that the sitter is currently pregnant. If the sitter is male, then the pomegranate can still indicate that someone close to him is pregnant. It can also represent that the time has come for the male sitter to start exploring the feminine side of their nature.

Symbol found in some of these cards

The High Priestess

Pool

Symbolises a fresh start.

Within a reading, a pool can indicate a desire on the sitter's part to 'cleanse' themselves, or to rid themselves of negative thoughts or emotions. The sitter needs to 'wash away' events of their recent past, so that they can restart their life and move on.

Symbol found in some of these cards
The King of Cups
The Nine of Coins

Pregnancy
Symbolises personal growth.
Within a reading, the appearance of a pregnant woman indicates that some aspect of the sitter's life is starting to grow or develop. This could represent the 'birth' or germ of an idea that is leading the sitter to follow a new path in life. Can also indicate the development of a new idea, or possibly a new goal in life that the sitter has set themselves.

(Hardly ever represents an actual pregnancy, although occasionally it can.)

Symbol found in some of these cards
The Empress

Chapter Fourteen
R

Rabbit

Symbolises being grounded.

Within a reading, rabbits are considered to be a strong spiritual symbol in the world of spiritualism. It can be regarded as a sign that the sitter is beginning to, or has already started to understand their spiritual needs, as opposed to their materialistic needs. This is probably manifesting itself in the sitters mind as understanding the importance of family and friends, for it is the people who are closest to us that keep us grounded in the real world.

Symbol found in some of these cards
The Queen of Coins

Rain

Symbolises renewal and regeneration.

Within a reading, rain is traditionally regarded as a sign of cleansing. For the sitter, this can be interpreted as a need to 'wash' away the old in order to embrace the new. Whatever is weighing down the sitter emotionally, now is the time to unburden themselves with the problems of the past and turn their heart to the future.

Symbol found in some of these cards
The Moon
The Three of Swords

Rainbow

Symbolises success and hope.

Within a reading, the shape of a rainbow can appear to resemble a bridge. This is significant for the sitter, as it implies that he or she has some bridges to build or repair in their life. This could be bridges in their professional or private lives. Now is the time to start, as the basic symbolism of a rainbow is success and joy.

Symbol found in some of these cards
The Seven of Cups
The Ten of Cups
The Four of Wands

Ram
Symbolises determination.
Within a reading, the appearance of a ram, or a ram's head indicates that the time has come for the sitter to take action and get themselves motivated in order to accomplish their goals. Whatever their goal in life is, it is not going to come along and drop itself in their lap. They must take responsibility, get up, get out there and start the process by themselves.

Symbol found in some of these cards
The Emperor
The Queen of Pentacles

Red Sky
Symbolises trouble ahead.
Within a reading, the red sky is not telling the sitter that tomorrow will be a nice day as the old saying goes. It appears in the spread as a warning of trouble ahead. The sitter may not know what this warning refers to, but now is the time for the sitter to anticipate the probable problem, or problems that are coming their way and to prepare for it.

Symbol found in some of these cards
The Seven of Coins
The Five of Wands
The Nine of Wands
The Knight of Wands

Reeds

Symbolises versatility.

Within a reading, the appearance of reeds indicates that the sitter might be experiencing confusion in their life. The rapidly growing, very adaptable and flexible reed, is a reminder to the sitter to rise above it all. Although the sitter's mind might be reeling with all the confusion that surrounds them at the moment, now is the time to rise above their conflicting emotions and see the bigger picture. The sitter needs a broader perspective in order to make sense of the confusion.

Symbol found in some of these cards
The Moon

Ribbons

Symbolises fragility.

Within a reading, ribbons should never be ignored, as they bring to our attention just how fragile the bonds that bind us really are. The sitter should take a good look at the relationships that they have with those who are closest to them. Are they treating their loved ones, their friends or colleagues with the respect that they deserve? If not, they could end up forcing then away.

Symbol found in some of these cards
The Two of Wands
The Eight of Wands

River

Symbolises obstacles.

Within a reading, the appearance of a river can be interpreted in two different ways. For the sitter, a river can represent an obstacle that they have to get across, as it is blocking their path or progress. On the other hand, it could be advising the sitter to stop struggling with whatever problem that they are facing or dealing with. It is time for them to 'go with the flow' and let the problem resolve itself.

<u>Symbol found in some of these cards</u>
Temperance
The Five of Cups
The Eight of Cups
The Ten of Cups
The Knight of Cups
The Four of Wands
The Eight of Wands

Rock

Symbolises dependability.

Within a reading, the appearance of a rock (or rocks) suggests that the sitter is one of life's more dependable souls. Their passion and determination is apparent in everything that they do. It shows that they have the personal strength to overcome the situations that life throws at them. The old sayings 'as solid as a rock' and 'he/she is my rock' definitely apply to this sitter.

<u>Symbol found in some of these cards</u>
The Four of Cups
The Five of Cups
The Seven of Wands

Ropes (Restraints)

Symbolises restriction.

Within a reading, the appearance of ropes, especially if being used to restrain someone, infers that the sitter is feeling restricted in some way. They might be experiencing a feeling of being trapped or helpless in their present situation. The sitter needs to relax, as the harder that they struggle against these symbolic ropes, the tighter they will become.

<u>Symbol found in some of these cards</u>
The Hanged Man
The Eight of Swords

Roses

Symbolises balance.

Within a reading, a rose, or roses, have always been associated with love, affection and relationships. For the sitter, they should remember that the rose represents promise and new beginnings. However, the sitter should be aware of the fact that the rose also has thorns. The thorns can represent possible painful ordeals along the way. As beautiful as a rose is, there is a balance to be struck.

Symbol found in some of these cards
The Fool
The Magician
Strength
Death
The Queen of Coins
The Two of Wands

Ruff (Collar)

Symbolises stiffness of attitude.

Within a reading, the ruff was a stiffly starched decorative collar worn by the Elizabethans who believed that it displayed their mastery over their bodily sensations. For the present day sitter however, the meaning is a little less pompous. It can simply represent the fact that the sitter is being a little 'stiff-necked' about something. The time has come for the sitter to relax a bit, let go and enjoy life more.

Symbol found in some of these cards
The Page of Swords
The Page of Wands

Chapter Fifteen
S

Scales

Symbolises balance.

Within a reading, scales have the fairly obvious meaning of balance. For the sitter however, the scales can represent that some aspect of their life is actually out of balance. Something in their life is throwing them out of kilter, so the sitter needs to identify the cause of this imbalance and take the required action in order to restore the equilibrium.

Symbol found in some of these cards
Justice
The Sun
The Six of Coins

Scorpion

Symbolises potential threats.

Within a reading, a scorpion is a strong spiritual sign that represents self-defence or protection. In a spread, it infers that the sitter needs to protect themselves from possible attack, guarding their flank and keep an eye on their blind spots. This is not a warning about physical attack, this is more in the area of an emotional attack or possibly slander. Keeping themselves aware in this way will protect the sitter from potential threats.

Symbol found in some of these cards
Death

Scroll

Symbolises learning.

Within a reading, the appearance of a scroll indicates that the sitter has achieved something recently. This could be an educational achievement or possibly a goal in life. In certain cases, a scroll can indicate that the sitter is unaware of something that is coming their way. In this case, the scroll indicates that the sitter needs to learn something, to educate themselves about this impending situation in order for them to be able to deal with it properly.

Symbol found in some of these cards
The High Priestess
Justice

Sea (Ocean)
Symbolises an unsettled time.

Within a reading, the appearance of the sea is designed to make us think about our life. The sitter should consider the vastness and the strength of the sea. It can be calm, but it can suddenly turn violent and unleash its power. For the sitter this can indicate that their life has recently been full of ups and downs, as situations ebb and flow through their recent daily routine. They probably feel as if they have recently been washed about from pillar to post. Calm will return, but they will have to be patient and ride out the storm.

Symbol found in some of these cards
The Two of Swords
The Five of Swords
The Six of Swords
The Eight of Swords
The Ten of Swords
The Ace of Cups
The Three of Cups
The Five of Cups
The Page of Cups
The Knight of Cups
The Queen of Cups
The King of Cups
The Two of Coins
The Two of Wands
The Three of Wands

The Page of Wands

Sea Horses
Symbolises grounding.

Within a reading, seahorses are beautiful, serene and graceful creatures. They make no attempt whatsoever to change themselves in order to adapt to their environment. In bad weather they simply curl their tail around something, staying where they are until the bad weather has passed. For the sitter this has the symbolic meaning of 'staying true to yourself'. It can also indicate that the sitter is one of those people who takes whatever life throws at them in their stride.

Symbol found in some of these cards
The King of Cups

Shells
Symbolises protection.

Within a reading, the appearance of any kind of shell can infer that the sitter is feeling a little vulnerable at the moment. This could be an emotional, financial or an employment situation that is causing the sitter worry. Whatever is causing trouble for the sitter, he or she needs to prepare for this situation and put a defensive barrier in place, a 'protective shell' to fend off whatever is happening to them at the moment, or for whatever is coming their way.

Symbol found in some of these cards
The Page of Cups
The King of Cups

Shelves
Symbolises storing knowledge.

Within a reading, a shelf or shelves represents the fact that the sitter is facing a decision, but that they are unprepared to make that decision. The shelves are empty at the moment and it is up to the sitter to carry out the necessary research and to acquire the information and the knowledge that they need to fill those shelves. This is the only way that the sitter can face that decision and settle on the correct outcome. Otherwise, the sitter runs the risk of getting it all wrong.

Symbol found in some of these cards
The Three of Coins

Shield
Symbolises protection.

Within a reading, the appearance of a shield represents that the sitter is in need of protecting themselves and those that they love from the harsh realities of life. No matter how happy, safe and secure they might feel at the moment, they should be deeply aware that they are as vulnerable as the rest of us. However, being aware of this vulnerability will allow them to prepare themselves in order to be ready to raise their protective shield whenever they need it.

Symbol found in some of these cards
The Empress
The Five of Swords
The Six of Wands

Skeleton (or Skull)
Symbolises transition.

Within a reading, while most of us look upon skulls and skeletons as a creepy reminder of our own mortality, they have a completely different meaning in the Tarot. For the sitter, a skull or a skeleton represents half-formed, or not fully developed ideas or plans. The sitter might be in the early stages of their project, but they can take comfort with the appearance of skulls or skeletons, as they represent change, transition or transformation, usually for the better.

<u>Symbol found in some of these cards</u>
Death

<u>Snail</u>
Symbolises steady progress.

Within a reading, a snail indicates that the sitter might be trying to rush things. Whatever goal that the sitter is aiming to achieve, they should realise that there is no shortcut. No matter how hard the sitter tries, their progress cannot be hurried. Success does not come overnight, but it will happen. The snail represents slow, but steady progress and the sitter will just have to learn to be a bit less impatient.

<u>Symbol found in some of these cards</u>
The Nine of Coins

<u>Snake</u>
Symbolises transformation.

Within a reading, a snake can symbolise renewal and rebirth, because it sheds its skin and re-emerges ready for its next phase in life. For the sitter, this can indicate that they should probably ask themselves if they need to 'shed' some part of themselves. Shedding some negative aspect of their life will allow them to grow and move on. A snake can also represent the fact that the sitter should be on the alert for so-called friends who really do not have their best interests at heart, a 'snake in the grass' so to speak.

<u>Symbol found in some of these cards</u>
The Magician
The Lovers
The Wheel of Fortune
The Seven of Cups

Snow (Snowflakes)

Symbolises a fresh start.

Within a reading, snow can have two interpretations. In the first instance, the sitter might be feeling that some important information is being kept from them. They might feel that they are getting the 'cold shoulder' or that they are being 'kept out in the cold' because something is being withheld. On the other hand, a blanket of snow can represent a fresh start, a whole new beginning, as the blanket of snow gives promise of the springtime to come.

Symbol found in some of these cards

The Five of Coins
The Seven of Wands
The Eight of Wands

Soldiers

Symbolises structure.

Within a reading, the appearance of a soldier or soldiers, indicates that the sitter is in need of some order in their life. Events are unfolding around them at a fast pace and everything seems chaotic to the sitter at the moment. They must discipline themselves to tackle each of their problems one by one, no matter what else is happening in the background. This is the only way that the sitter can sort out the chaos and bring structure back into their life.

Symbol found in some of these cards

The Five of Swords

Sphinx

Symbolises mystery.

Within a reading, the ancient Sphinx represents the keeper of secrets and the mysteries of life. For the sitter this implies that they are trying to solve a riddle or mystery in their life. This usually consists of some information that has come their way, which is causing them some confusion. The sitter will have to dig deep and/or carry out some research in order to solve this mystery.

Symbol found in some of these cards
The Chariot
The Wheel of Fortune

Spider
Symbolises resilience.

Within a reading, the industrious spider will build and rebuild its web, no matter how many times it is destroyed by the elements. For the sitter this can represent that they are trying to achieve a goal in their life, but that they are constantly being knocked back or blocked in some way. No matter what, in order to achieve their goal, the sitter must never give up. Try, try and try again – they will get there in the end.

Symbol found in some of these cards
Death
The Eight of Swords

Stag
Symbolises quiet strength.

Within a reading, the appearance of the noble stag is an indication that the sitter might be holding back in some aspect of their life. Although this usually refers to a work matter, it can also relate to a relationship or family matter. Whether it be a professional or private matter, the stag is a sign telling the sitter that the time has come to stand tall and make your presence felt, rather than staying in the background.

Symbol found in some of these cards
The Empress

Stained Glass
Symbolises your outlook.

Within a reading, when stained glass appears in the spread, it is often regarded as the spiritual window to the soul. For the sitter however, it is a sign that the time has come to start being honest with themselves about a situation that is unfolding around them. They must ask themselves if they are looking at this situation clearly, or are they looking at it through 'rose coloured glasses'?

Symbol found in some of these cards
Temperance
The Four of Swords
The Five of Coins

Stairway
Symbolises a new path or goal.

Within a reading, a stairway can often suggest that the sitter is about to start on a whole new path in life. This could simply be the first tentative step on the ladder to a new career, or the beginning of a new goal that the sitter has set for themselves. It can also represent that the sitter has started to take their own spirituality to another level. For example, they might be starting to become aware of their own psychic abilities and that they have started to explore the possibilities.

Symbol found in some of these cards
The Seven of Wands

Star (Stars)
Symbolises guidance.

Within a reading, the appearance of stars in the spread indicates that the sitter is experiencing some turmoil in their life at the moment. Their life seems to be a little topsy-turvy right now, causing them a lot of confusion. The star symbol deals with shedding some light into their life. They must focus on one problem at a time and deal with it, moving onto the next problem and dealing with that and so on. There is light at the end of the tunnel, but the illumination of that light comes from within.

Symbol found in some of these cards
The Empress
The Chariot
The Star
The Seven of Cups
The Three of Coins

Sun
Symbolises life and rebirth.

Within a reading, just as the sun rises every morning, so a new day begins for the sitter. The position of the sun in a Tarot card is also significant. A rising sun promises new beginnings, while a setting sun infers that something is coming to an end. A full mid-day sun indicates energy, strength and success in creative endeavours.

Symbol found in some of these cards
The Fool
Death
Temperance
The Sun
The Six of Wands
The Page of Wands

Sunflower
Symbolises positivity.

Within a reading, because sunflowers are such 'happy' flowers, they brighten up the lives of all who look at them. For the sitter however, it can imply that they are feeling a little down, in the doldrums so to speak. The sunflower is urging the sitter to stop looking at the dark side of their situation, as focusing on what is wrong in their life will only depress them more. They should start looking at the lighter side of life, as concentrating on the good or happy things in life will lift their mood.

Symbol found in some of these cards
The Sun
The Queen of Wands

Sunrise
Symbolises a new beginning.

Within a reading, the image of a sunrise, or dawn, infers that the sitter is about to enter a new phase in their life. This could be the beginning of a new venture, a new project or possibly even the start of a new relationship. It also heralds a real chance for happiness, so the sitter should embrace this new start just as they would embrace a new day.

Symbol found in some of these cards
The Ace of Wands

Sunset
Symbolises an ending.

Within a reading, the image of a sunset infers that some aspect of the sitter's life is winding down or coming to an end. This could be a period of intense work, a difficult phase, a troubling time or maybe just the end of a project that has taken longer to complete than anticipated. Whatever it is that is coming to an end, it is now time for the sitter to relax, as the worst is now over.

Symbol found in some of these cards
The Six of Cups
The Two of Wands
The Three of Wands
The Nine of Wands

Swan

Symbolises loyalty.

Within a reading, the appearance of a swan signifies that dignity and loyalty has (or is about to) come into their life. This could be in the shape of a professional advancement, but it is more likely to be within a new relationship. The swan also suggests that now is the time for the sitter to trust their instincts and to go with their gut feeling.

Symbol found in some of these cards
The Empress

Sword

Symbolises defending oneself.

Within a reading, the interpretation of a sword symbol is as two-edged as the sword itself. On one hand, the sword can indicate that the sitter feels threatened in some way. Whether at work or within the sitter's personal life, they feel the need to fight back or to defend themselves. On the other hand, a sword can also indicate that it is the sitter who is the aggressor. They might be forcing their view or opinion on others, upsetting them and making them feel they must defend themselves against the sitter.
(Note – this interpretation cannot be used for any card from the Suit of Swords in general, unless more than two cards from that suit appear in the spread.)

Symbol found in some of these cards
The Magician
Justice

Chapter Sixteen
T

Tassels

Symbolises achievement.

Within a reading, as tassels have always been associated with power, position and prestige, they are a good sign for the sitter. They foretell the achievement of desires or goals and as such, are a sign of success. They can also represent victory, or success over whatever hardships that the sitter is currently facing at the moment. If they stay resolute, they will overcome those hardships and come through it all successfully.

Symbol found in some of these cards
The Nine of Swords
The Knight of Swords
The Two of Cups
The Knight of Cups
The Page of Wands

Teardrops

Symbolises sorrows.

Within a reading, the appearance of teardrops within a spread indicates that the sitter is going through a painful process of some description at the moment. This could be anything from the recent loss of a loved one, up to being plagued with painful memories of an incident from their past. It might take time, but the sitter will get over these sorrows. They can speed up the process if they can learn how to alter the way that they think.

Symbol found in some of these cards
The Three of Swords
The Five of Cups

Tents (Marquees)

Symbolises refuge.

Within a reading, a tent can represent a temporary refuge from the hustle and bustle of life. For the sitter it can indicate that life is starting to get them down and that they are looking for an escape. It should be pointed out that a tent is a temporary structure, which indicates that the difficulties that the sitter is experiencing right now are as temporary as the tent itself.

Symbol found in some of these cards

The Seven of Swords

Throne

Symbolises stability.

Within a reading, as a throne is a seat of authority, this represents a position of responsibility for the sitter. Some aspect of the sitter's life is completely under their control. This could be a position at work, as in a managerial post. Possibly at home where the sitter has sole responsibility for raising a child or caring for someone for example. Whichever aspect of the sitter's life the throne refers to, it is running smoothly, but only because of the sitter's determination and steady hand.

Symbol found in some of these cards

The Empress
The Emperor
Justice
The Queen of Swords
The King of Swords
The Queen of Cups
The King of Cups
The Queen of Coins
The King of Coins
The Queen of Wands
The King of Wands

Tomb

Symbolises freeing yourself.

Within a reading, the appearance of a tomb never represents physical death. Instead, it indicates that the time has come for the sitter to 'lay to rest' any thoughts or memories that are troubling them. Freeing themselves from those troubling thoughts or memories will allow the sitter to escape from a period of mental stagnation. This will set them free to start a new phase of understanding that will improve their life.

Symbol found in some of these cards

Judgement

The Four of Swords

Tools

Symbolises reshaping your life.

Within a reading, the appearance of one, or a collection of tools is an indication that the sitter is doing something wrong. Whatever path that the sitter is following is either the wrong path for them, or that they are following the correct path incorrectly. The time has come for the sitter to gather the tools that they need (possibly tools that they have never considered before) in order to 'reshape' their path in life. In this case, the tools that the sitter needs are information, research and a lot of soul searching.

Symbol found in some of these cards

The Three of Coins

The Eight of Coins

Tornado

Symbolises loss of control.

Within a reading, a tornado really isn't a good sign, as it represents upheaval in the sitter's life. This could be the sitter feeling overwhelmed by current events. Or possibly a feeling of losing control over their present situation. Whatever aspect of the sitter's life is going wrong for them, they are feeling that their life is spinning out of control and probably they are feeling a little helpless about it all. Now is the time for the sitter to take an in depth look at their situation and to take the necessary steps to regain control.

Symbol found in some of these cards
The Knight of Swords

Tower

Symbolises sanctuary.

Within a reading, a tower represents sanctuary, a safe place that we can retreat to when things get too much for us. This safe place can simply be within our own minds, possibly just reliving old memories that bring us a degree of comfort. Anybody can take their mind away from the pressures of life by daydreaming for example. On the other hand, the tower can represent an actual physical location where the sitter feels safe and relaxed, usually their own home. In the Tower Card, the tower is being damaged by lightening. This can imply that the sitter's 'safe place' is under threat in some way.

Symbol found in some of these cards
The Tower
The Moon

Treasure Box

Symbolises secrets.

Within a reading, a treasure box implies that the sitter is keeping something to themselves. This could be a memory of something that has happened to the sitter that they wish to keep secret. It could be information about someone or something that they have been entrusted with and that they know they must never reveal. If this is a sentimental memory, then they should keep it close to their heart and cherish it. On the other hand, if this memory relates to something nasty that has happened, then now is the time to seek help.

Symbol found in some of these cards
The Ten of Coins
The Two of Wands

Trees
Symbolises growth.

Within a reading, trees appear in many of the Tarot Cards, but significantly, they usually appear in the background. If trees appear in a lot of the cards within a spread, then this indicates that the sitter has plans for a new venture, path or phase in their life. However, at the moment, these plans are at the back of the sitter's mind. These plans are something that the sitter is considering putting into action in the near future, as they are still working on them, costing them out or carrying out research.

Symbol found in some of these cards
The Empress
The Lovers
The Wheel of Fortune
The Hanged Man
The Tower
The Star
The Five of Swords
The Six of Swords
The Page of Swords
The Knight of Swords
The Queen of Swords
The King of Swords
The Four of Cups
The Ten of Cups
The Knight of Cups
The King of Cups
The Nine of Coins
The Page of Coins
The Knight of Coins
The Ace of Wands

The Four of Wands
The Five of Wands
The Eight of Wands
The Ten of Wands
The Knight of Wands

Triangle
Symbolises strength.

Within a reading, the triangle is the strongest basic geometric shape known to man, which is why it is used to support a roof in a domestic building for example. It is this very strength of the triangle which is significant in a reading. It infers that the sitter has a strong character, as in moral strength rather than physical strength. Whatever life throws at this particular sitter, they can handle it.

Symbol found in some of these cards
Temperance
The Ace of Swords
The Page of Cups
The Six of Wands
The Ten of Wands
The Page of Wands

Trumpet (Horn)
Symbolises announcement.

Within a reading, horns represent a joyous or triumphant period in the sitter's life. The sitter has something to shout about, something that they need to tell the world about – but not quite yet. They are waiting for the right time to make their happy announcement. Although filled with excitement, the sitter will know when the time is just right to announce their happy news of what has happened, or what it is that is about to happen.

Symbol found in some of these cards
Judgement

Chapter Seventeen
V & W

Veil

Symbolises mysticism.

Within a reading, a veil can represent two sides of the same coin. On the one hand, a veil can indicate that the sitter is hiding behind a façade, not allowing the world to see the real person inside. On the other hand, a veil can represent that the sitter possesses hidden knowledge, usually of a spiritual or psychic nature. Either way, the sitter sits behind a veil of mysticism and is usually an old soul with life experiences beyond their years.

Symbol found in some of these cards

The High Priestess
The Seven of Cups
The Queen of Wands

Wall

Symbolises barriers.

Within a reading, a wall represents building a barrier in life. For the sitter, this refers to them needing to separate one area of their life from another. The surrounding cards should give an indication as to what areas need separating. It can also suggest that the sitter is holding back in some way, hiding behind a wall of their own making. However, a wall can also suggest quite simply that the sitter is in need of some privacy.

Symbol found in some of these cards

The Sun
The Five of Cups
The Six of Cups
The King of Coins
The Two of Wands

Water

Symbolises cleansing.

Within a reading, water usually represents the need for the sitter to 'cleanse' themselves. Not in the physical sense of needing a wash, but in an emotional or spiritual sense. In other words, the sitter needs to 'wash away' whatever it is that is troubling them. This would normally be an old memory, experience or episode in their life that is holding the sitter back. Once they have removed the issues that are bothering them, they will feel reborn and ready to move on with their life.

Symbol found in some of these cards

The Temperance
The Star
The Moon
Judgement
The Ace of Cups
The Two of Cups
The King of Cups
The Two of Coins

Waterfall

Symbolises letting go.

Within a reading, a waterfall indicates that the time has come for the sitter to rid themselves (to let go) of something that is holding them back. This could be events in their past, some negative thoughts or some belief that used to be very important to them. Just as the waterfall sweeps away all of the detritus that it encounters along its way, the sitter should do the same. Letting go of these emotions, worries or memories will set them free to enjoy a new and uncluttered phase in their life.

Symbol found in some of these cards

The Empress
The Eight of Cups

Wheat

Symbolises abundance.

Within a reading, the appearance of wheat indicates a period of growth, renewal and abundance. A wheat field is a thing of beauty to behold, conjuring up images of golden summers and happy childhood memories. For the sitter, this implies that they have entered, or are about to enter a 'golden' phase in their life. All of the sitter's hard work, planning and/or patience is about to be rewarded.

Symbol found in some of these cards
The Seven of Coins

Wheel

Symbolises cycles.

Within a reading, a wheel represents different things depending on the surrounding cards. It can refer to the cycle of life, so possibly the sitter has recently experienced a birth and a death within their family group. It can also infer that the sitter is caught in a cycle of events that is causing them some difficulty and that they are really trying very hard to break free from that cycle. Lastly, it can represent that the sitter feels stuck in a repetitive cycle of work and sleep, and that they are trying to figure out a new path for themselves – possibly a new hobby for example.

Symbol found in some of these cards
The Wheel of Fortune

Window

Symbolises a new outlook.

Within a reading, a window represents a new perspective, or a new opportunity. However, it can also indicate that the sitter feels as if they are on the outside looking in. The time has come for the sitter to move inside and take an active part in whatever it is that they have been observing. Only by joining in will they be able to take advantage of all the new opportunities that will be within their grasp.

Symbol found in some of these cards
The Four of Swords
The Seven of Swords
The Nine of Swords
The Three of Coins
The Five of Coins
The Eight of Coins

Wings
Symbolises freedom.
Within a reading, wings represent a desire to be free. For the sitter, this could mean that they need the freedom to express themselves properly, or to act more freely in their life. It can also represent the need on the sitter's part to break free from whatever constraints that are holding them back at the moment. If the wings are detached from the bird and attached to something else, this can infer that the sitter is being held back in some way. Someone or something has 'clipped their wings'.
(If the wings are attached to an Angel, please go to the Angel Wings entry.)

Symbol found in some of these cards
The High Priestess
The Empress
The Knight of Swords
The Queen of Swords
The King of Swords
The Two of Cups
The Knight of Cups

Wolf

Symbolises loyalty.

Within a reading, the appearance of a wolf can indicate that the sitter's loyalties are being tested in some way. This could be a situation that has arisen at work, or within the sitter's circle of family and friends. The loyal and intelligent wolf reminds us that we do not have to 'follow the pack' or to try and 'fit in'. The sitter must be true to themselves and follow their heart when deciding where their loyalties lie.

Symbol found in some of these cards

The Wheel of Fortune

The Moon

Workbench

Symbolises creativity.

Within a reading, the appearance of a workbench indicates that the sitter is going through a busy time right now, or is possibly just about to begin a busy period in their life. The workbench hints at hard work, industrious efforts and creativity. The sitter must work hard to achieve the goals that they have set for themselves, but this is not an issue for them. They are ready, willing and able with all of the tools that they need at hand, in order to achieve that goal.

Symbol found in some of these cards

The Eight of Coins

Chapter Eighteen
Y & Z

Yellow Flowers

Symbolises friendship.

Within a reading, any yellow flower is regarded as a symbol of the bonds of friendship that exist in our lives. For the sitter, apart from indicating friendship, yellow flowers can also be a sign that they have enjoyed some success recently. Lastly, the bright and sunny colour of a yellow flower can also indicate that the sitter is one of life's optimists, always seeing the good in people and events.

Symbol found in some of these cards

The Sun

Yin Yang

Symbolises balance.

Within a reading, the appearance of the yin-yang symbol can be interpreted in different ways. The surrounding cards will indicate which interpretation applies to the sitter. It infers that the sitter is trying to achieve some balance in their life, or that possibly they have recently achieved the balance that they seek. This symbol can also imply that the sitter is being drawn in two different directions by some seemingly opposite or contrary forces that might actually be complementary and interconnected. The old saying of 'opposites attract' springs to mind.

Symbol found in some of these cards

The Chariot

Justice

Zodiac Circle

Symbolises our circle of friends.

Within a reading, the appearance of the zodiac circle comes as a reminder that we do not live our lives alone. We are surrounded by people from the other star signs and we are influenced by the character of the animals that some of them represent. For the sitter, if they are struggling a little at the moment, then they should turn to their 'circle' of family and friends for help, just as they would turn to the sitter in their hour of need if they had to.

<u>Symbol found in some of these cards</u>
The Wheel of Fortune
The World
The Ace of Swords

Part Two

00 The Fool

Cliff Edge

Signifies possible new opportunities.

Within a reading, a cliff edge can represent two things. The sitter is about to embark on a new path, which has been created by the arrival of a new opportunity in their life. On one hand, this is an exciting time for the sitter. On the other hand, they should take precautions, as there are potential pitfalls ahead.

Dog/Dogs

Symbolises loyalty or devotion.

Within a reading, whenever a dog (or dogs) appear in the spread it represents that the sitter might be experiencing loyalty issues. However, a dog can also represent that the sitter is on the right track in life, as dogs are symbolic of stability and steadfastness.

Earth (The Planet)

Symbolises Nature (as in Mother Earth) fertility and life.

Within a reading, the appearance of planet Earth indicates that the sitter has a keen affinity with nature and the natural world. As the Earth is a sphere, this can also indicate that the sitter is currently experiencing completeness in some aspect of their life.

Ice

Symbolises difficult territory.

Within a reading, ice usually appears on mountaintops in the background of a card. This suggests that the sitter knows within themselves (at the back of their minds) that they need to calm down (cool it) and react less to a negative situation that they are facing.

Mountains

Symbolises challenges.

Within a reading, mountains usually appear in the background of the card. For the sitter, this suggests that they are facing seemingly insurmountable challenges, but that the sitter is trying to ignore them, pushing them to the back of their mind. If mountains appear in the majority of the spread, this indicates that the time has come for the sitter to face those challenges and to deal with them.

Roses

Symbolises balance.

Within a reading, a rose, or roses, have always been associated with love, affection and relationships. For the sitter, they should remember that the rose represents promise and new beginnings. However, the sitter should be aware of the fact that the rose also has thorns. The thorns can represent possible painful ordeals along the way. As beautiful as a rose is, there is a balance to be struck.

Sun

Symbolises life and rebirth.

Within a reading, just as the sun rises every morning, so a new day begins for the sitter. The position of the sun in a Tarot card is also significant. A rising sun promises new beginnings, while a setting sun infers that something is coming to an end. A full mid-day sun indicates energy, strength and success in creative endeavours.

01 The Magician

Baton

Symbolises spiritual authority or the development of ideas.

Within a reading, the baton represents the need of the sitter to take control of some aspect of the life, to be more authoritative in their dealings with others.

Infinity Symbol

Symbolises endless possibilities.

Within a reading, the Infinity Symbol (The Lemniscate) represents the never-ending possibilities in our lives. For the sitter, it implies that they possess the necessary endless energy to face whatever life throws at them. It can also represent everlasting love.

Library

Symbolises knowledge.

Within a reading, the appearance of a library, or a collection of books, relates to the gathering together of knowledge and/or wisdom. For the sitter, books can indicate a period of study that they are going through or that they are about to begin. This study and gathering of knowledge bodes well for the sitter, as it will open new doors for them.

Lilies

Symbolises purity, love and relationships.

Within a reading, the appearance of a lily, or lilies, refers to a period of personal growth and development for the sitter. The lily can also indicate that the sitter (or someone that they are close to) is about to embark on a new relationship or that there is a birth in their immediate future.

Roses

Symbolises balance.

Within a reading, a rose, or roses, have always been associated with love, affection and relationships. For the sitter, they should remember that the rose represents promise and new beginnings. However, the sitter should be aware of the fact that the rose also has thorns. The thorns can represent possible painful ordeals along the way. As beautiful as a rose is, there is a balance to be struck.

Snake

Symbolises transformation.

Within a reading, a snake can symbolise renewal and rebirth, because it sheds its skin and re-emerges ready for its next phase in life. For the sitter, this can indicate that they should probably ask themselves if they need to 'shed' some part of themselves. Shedding some negative aspect of their life will allow them to grow and move on. A snake can also represent the fact that the sitter should be on the alert for so-called friends who really do not have their best interests at heart, a 'snake in the grass' so to speak.

Sword

Symbolises defending oneself.

Within a reading, the interpretation of a sword symbol is as two-edged as the sword itself. On one hand, the sword can indicate that the sitter feels threatened in some way. Whether at work or within the sitter's personal life, they feel the need to fight back or to defend themselves. On the other hand, a sword can also indicate that it is the sitter who is the aggressor. They might be forcing their view or opinion on others, upsetting them and making them feel they must defend themselves against the sitter.

(Note – this interpretation cannot be used for any card from the Suit of Swords in general, unless more than two cards from that suit appear in the spread.)

02 The High Priestess

Moon

Symbolises cycles.

Within a reading, the appearance of the moon in a spread indicates that the sitter is moving from one phase of their life to another. Whatever transition is taking place in the sitter's life, it is for the sitter's overall good and/or wellbeing. The moon can also indicate that the sitter is quite a spiritual person, who might very well be starting to realise that they have psychic abilities themselves.

Owl

Symbolises wisdom.

Within a reading, an owl can be interpreted in two ways. It can represent the fact that the sitter needs to 'wisen up' to the circumstances that presently surround them. However, it can also mean that the sitter already possesses the required wisdom to deal with whatever they have been confronted with recently. The surrounding cards will indicate which interpretation applies.

Pillar

Symbolises stability.

Within a reading, a pillar or pillars, represent strength, stability and balance. A single pillar can suggest that the sitter is the one who is supporting those around them, as in 'a pillar of strength'. When two pillars appear, usually at each side of the card, this could indicate that the sitter should consider their problems in a more diplomatic, or balanced way. Rather than left or right or black and white, the sitter should try to consider a more central view. In other words, the sitter should adopt a new perspective, a middle-of-the-road approach when tackling their problems.

Pomegranate

Symbolises femininity.

Within a reading, the pomegranate is a symbol in many cultures that represents love, marriage and fertility. A pomegranate could infer that the sitter is thinking about starting a family, or possibly that the sitter is currently pregnant. If the sitter is male, then the pomegranate can still indicate that someone close to him is pregnant. It can also represent that the time has come for the male sitter to start exploring the feminine side of their nature.

Scroll

Symbolises learning.

Within a reading, the appearance of a scroll indicates that the sitter has achieved something recently. This could be an educational achievement or possibly a goal in life. In certain cases, a scroll can indicate that the sitter is unaware of something that is coming their way. In this case, the scroll indicates that the sitter needs to learn something, to educate themselves about this impending situation in order for them to be able to deal with it properly.

Veil

Symbolises mysticism.

Within a reading, a veil can represent two sides of the same coin. On the one hand, a veil can indicate that the sitter is hiding behind a façade, not allowing the world to see the real person inside. On the other hand, a veil can represent that the sitter possesses hidden knowledge, usually of a spiritual or psychic nature. Either way, the sitter sits behind a veil of mysticism and is usually an old soul with life experiences beyond their years.

Wings

Symbolises freedom.

Within a reading, wings represent a desire to be free. For the sitter, this could mean that they need the freedom to express themselves properly, or to act more freely in their life. It can also represent the need on the sitter's part to break free from whatever constraints that are holding them back at the moment. If the wings are detached from the bird and attached to something else, this can infer that the sitter is being held back in some way. Someone or something has 'clipped their wings'.

(If the wings are attached to an Angel, please go to the Angel Wings entry.)

03 The Empress

Arch

Symbolises new beginnings.

Within a reading, the arch suggests that the sitter is about to take a new direction in life – whether they know it or not. A new opportunity is about to present itself to the sitter. This could be a new opening at work, a new career path for them to follow or possibly a new romantic involvement.

Butterfly

Symbolises transformation.

Within a reading, a butterfly suggests that it is time for the sitter to move away from their currant phase in life to another, better phase. It can also represent that the sitter will have to change their way of thinking if they want to achieve their goals in life.

Corn

Symbolises fertility and rebirth.

Within a reading, sheaves of corn, or a whole cornfield, can represent that the sitter's mind is alive with ideas for their future. It is an exciting time for them as they plan out their new path in life. Corn can also represent fertility, pregnancy or childbirth.

Crown

Symbolises authority and power.

Within a reading, the appearance of a crown can signify many things. It could suggest that the sitter needs authority in their life. Possibly that the sitter desires recognition for their achievements. Or even that the sitter desires more control of their life, which might feel a little out of control to them at the moment.

Flowers

Symbolises new life and regeneration.

Within a reading, different individual flowers have different meanings. However, flowers in general represent that the sitter is opening (or has already opened) themselves up to new ideas, beliefs or experiences, all of which they will benefit from.

Leopard

Symbolises strength.

Within a reading, the leopard infers that the sitter needs to start trusting their inner self a lot more, as they possess a strength of character that they seem to be unaware of. A leopard can also represent a period of renewal for the sitter, as in 'changing your spots'. It is during this period of renewal that the sitter will need to draw on their inner strength to see it through to its successful end.

Mouse

Symbolises scrutiny.

Within a reading, a mouse represents examination. As mice are pretty short-sighted, they have to examine their surroundings with great care. For the sitter, this suggests that they must pay attention to detail. If they are faced with legal documents or a contract for example, they must scrutinise that document and examine every detail before they sign it. Failure to do so could result in future problems.

Pregnancy

Symbolises personal growth.

Within a reading, the appearance of a pregnant woman indicates that some aspect of the sitter's life is starting to grow or develop. This could represent the 'birth' or germ of an idea that is leading the sitter to follow a new path in life. Can also indicate the development of a new idea, or possibly a new goal in life that the sitter has set themselves.

(Hardly ever represents an actual pregnancy, although occasionally it can.)

Shield

Symbolises protection.

Within a reading, the appearance of a shield represents that the sitter is in need of protecting themselves and those that they love from the harsh realities of life. No matter how happy, safe and secure they might feel at the moment, they should be deeply aware that they are as vulnerable as the rest of us. However, being aware of this vulnerability will allow them to prepare themselves in order to be ready to raise their protective shield whenever they need it.

Stag

Symbolises quiet strength.

Within a reading, the appearance of the noble stag is an indication that the sitter might be holding back in some aspect of their life. Although this usually refers to a work matter, it can also relate to a relationship or family matter. Whether it be a professional or private matter, the stag is a sign telling the sitter that the time has come to stand tall and make your presence felt, rather than staying in the background.

Star (Stars)

Symbolises guidance.

Within a reading, the appearance of stars in the spread indicates that the sitter is experiencing some turmoil in their life at the moment. Their life seems to be a little topsy-turvy right now, causing them a lot of confusion. The star symbol deals with shedding some light into their life. They must focus on one problem at a time and deal with it, moving onto the next problem and dealing with that and so on. There is light at the end of the tunnel, but the illumination of that light comes from within.

Swan

Symbolises loyalty.

Within a reading, the appearance of a swan signifies that dignity and loyalty has (or is about to) come into their life. This could be in the shape of a professional advancement, but it is more likely to be within a new relationship. The swan also suggests that now is the time for the sitter to trust their instincts and to go with their gut feeling.

Throne

Symbolises stability.

Within a reading, as a throne is a seat of authority, this represents a position of responsibility for the sitter. Some aspect of the sitter's life is completely under their control. This could be a position at work, as in a managerial post. Possibly at home where the sitter has sole responsibility for raising a child or caring for someone for example. Whichever aspect of the sitter's life the throne refers to, it is running smoothly, but only because of the sitter's determination and steady hand.

Trees

Symbolises growth.

Within a reading, trees appear in many of the Tarot Cards, but significantly, they usually appear in the background. If trees appear in a lot of the cards within a spread, then this indicates that the sitter has plans for a new venture, path or phase in their life. However, at the moment, these plans are at the back of the sitter's mind. These plans are something that the sitter is considering putting into action in the near future, as they are still working on them, costing them out or carrying out research.

Waterfall

Symbolises letting go.

Within a reading, a waterfall indicates that the time has come for the sitter to rid themselves (to let go) of something that is holding them back. This could be events in their past, some negative thoughts or some belief that used to be very important to them. Just as the waterfall sweeps away all of the detritus that it encounters along its way, the sitter should do the same. Letting go of these emotions, worries or memories will set them free to enjoy a new and uncluttered phase in their life.

Wings

Symbolises freedom.

Within a reading, wings represent a desire to be free. For the sitter, this could mean that they need the freedom to express themselves properly, or to act more freely in their life. It can also represent the need on the sitter's part to break free from whatever constraints that are holding them back at the moment. If the wings are detached from the bird and attached to something else, this can infer that the sitter is being held back in some way. Someone or something has 'clipped their wings'.

(If the wings are attached to an Angel, please go to the Angel Wings entry.)

04 The Emperor

Ankh

Symbolises life. (The Ankh is an Egyptian symbol)

Within a reading, the appearance of the Ankh means that there is a good balance within the sitter's life at the moment. This could refer to a good balance in their relationship, their emotional state, their occupation or maybe even their finances.

Pillar

Symbolises stability.

Within a reading, a pillar or pillars, represent strength, stability and balance. A single pillar can suggest that the sitter is the one who is supporting those around them, as in 'a pillar of strength'. When two pillars appear, usually at each side of the card, this could indicate that the sitter should consider their problems in a more diplomatic, or balanced way. Rather than left or right or black and white, the sitter should try to consider a more central view. In other words, the sitter should adopt a new perspective, a middle-of-the-road approach when tackling their problems.

Armour

Symbolises protection and strength.

Within a reading, the appearance of armour suggests that the sitter is feeling vulnerable in some way and that they feel the need to protect themselves from their perceived threat.

Crown

Symbolises authority and power.

Within a reading, the appearance of a crown can signify many things. It could suggest that the sitter needs authority in their life. Possibly that the sitter desires recognition for their achievements. Or even that the sitter desires more control of their life, which might feel a little out of control to them at the moment.

Crystal Ball or Glass Globe

Symbolises enlightenment.

Within a reading, a crystal ball or glass globe implies that the sitter is in need for clarity and focus in their life. Some aspect of their life is causing them great confusion. They need to know what it is that they want (or do not want) in life. Once they have figured this out, their path ahead will become clearer.

Eagle

Symbolises a connection to spiritual powers, Spirit Guides and Teachers.

Within a reading, the appearance of an eagle is a really good sign for any sitter who is trying to develop their psychic ability. It represents the fact that the sitter is doing well in their studies and that they will soon rise to the elevated heights that they are trying to achieve.

Globe

Symbolises achievement.

Within a reading, globes are sometimes shown as crystal balls or as the world, both of which are round in shape. Any round object or circle represents completion. This refers to the fact that the sitter is about to achieve some goal in their life. It is a sign of completion and infers that the sitter has the 'world at their fingertips'.

Mountains

Symbolises challenges.

Within a reading, mountains usually appear in the background of the card. For the sitter, this suggests that they are facing seemingly insurmountable challenges, but that the sitter is trying to ignore them, pushing them to the back of their mind. If mountains appear in the majority of the spread, this indicates that the time has come for the sitter to face those challenges and to deal with them.

Ram

Symbolises determination.

Within a reading, the appearance of a ram, or a ram's head indicates that the time has come for the sitter to take action and get themselves motivated in order to accomplish their goals. Whatever their goal in life is, it is not going to come along and drop itself in their lap. They must take responsibility, get up, get out there and start the process by themselves.

Throne

Symbolises stability.

Within a reading, as a throne is a seat of authority, this represents a position of responsibility for the sitter. Some aspect of the sitter's life is completely under their control. This could be a position at work, as in a managerial post. Possibly at home where the sitter has sole responsibility for raising a child or caring for someone for example. Whichever aspect of the sitter's life the throne refers to, it is running smoothly, but only because of the sitter's determination and steady hand.

05 The Hierophant

Crossed Keys

Symbolises the opening of new doors.

Within a reading, crossed keys as shown on the Hierophant, represent the keys to heaven, as held by Saint Peter. However, within a tarot card spread, any key, however it is presented, represents the opening of a new door in the sitter's life.

Crown

Symbolises authority and power.

Within a reading, the appearance of a crown can signify many things. It could suggest that the sitter needs authority in their life. Possibly that the sitter desires recognition for their achievements. Or even that the sitter desires more control of their life, which might feel a little out of control to them at the moment.

Key

Symbolises unlocking potential.

Within a reading, a key usually represents the fact that the sitter is about to unlock a hidden talent, or that they are about to open a new door (new path) in their life. Depending on the sitter's circumstances, a key can also represent closing a door on some part of their life, as in something coming to an end for the sitter.

Pillar

Symbolises stability.

Within a reading, a pillar or pillars, represent strength, stability and balance. A single pillar can suggest that the sitter is the one who is supporting those around them, as in 'a pillar of strength'. When two pillars appear, usually at each side of the card, this could indicate that the sitter should consider their problems in a more diplomatic, or balanced way. Rather than left or right or black and white, the sitter should try to consider a more central view. In other words, the sitter should adopt a new perspective, a middle-of-the-road approach when tackling their problems.

06 The Lovers

Angels

Symbolises divine messengers.

Within a reading, the appearance of an Angel in the spread represents that some kind of important information is coming the sitter's way. This could manifest itself in some sort of inspirational way, or even in a 'light bulb' moment. However the sitter receives this important information, they must not ignore it.

Angel Wings

Symbolises protection, affection, hope and happiness.

Within a reading, a pair of Angel wings on their own simply represents that some aspect of the sitter's life is going well. Even if they are unhappy with recent developments, they should be encouraged to concentrate on the good things that have happened and that are still going on around them.

Apple

Symbolises love, joy or knowledge.

Within a reading, the appearance of an apple suggests that the sitter is about to 'take a bite' out of that apple. This could represent the sitter is about to begin a new relationship, or that they are about to begin a new course of study.

Clouds

Symbolises transition.

Within a reading, clouds have different meanings depending on what colour they are. In the suit of Swords, most of the clouds are dark and fast moving, representing that the sitter is probably going through a troublesome (or stormy) period in their life. However, dark clouds like these can also represent confusion, or clouded judgement.

Heart

Symbolises love, joy and affection.

Within a reading, a heart suggests that the sitter needs to pay attention to the things that are important to them. The heart is also a symbol of truth, courage and loyalty. In that respect, it is probably time for the sitter to take stock of other people in their life, in order to see if these issues are reciprocated.

Mountains

Symbolises challenges.

Within a reading, mountains usually appear in the background of the card. For the sitter, this suggests that they are facing seemingly insurmountable challenges, but that the sitter is trying to ignore them, pushing them to the back of their mind. If mountains appear in the majority of the spread, this indicates that the time has come for the sitter to face those challenges and to deal with them.

Pillar

Symbolises stability.

Within a reading, a pillar or pillars, represent strength, stability and balance. A single pillar can suggest that the sitter is the one who is supporting those around them, as in 'a pillar of strength'. When two pillars appear, usually at each side of the card, this could indicate that the sitter should consider their problems in a more diplomatic, or balanced way. Rather than left or right or black and white, the sitter should try to consider a more central view. In other words, the sitter should adopt a new perspective, a middle-of-the-road approach when tackling their problems.

Snake

Symbolises transformation.

Within a reading, a snake can symbolise renewal and rebirth, because it sheds its skin and re-emerges ready for its next phase in life. For the sitter, this can indicate that they should probably ask themselves if they need to 'shed' some part of themselves. Shedding some negative aspect of their life will allow them to grow and move on. A snake can also represent the fact that the sitter should be on the alert for so-called friends who really do not have their best interests at heart, a 'snake in the grass' so to speak.

Trees

Symbolises growth.

Within a reading, trees appear in many of the Tarot Cards, but significantly, they usually appear in the background. If trees appear in a lot of the cards within a spread, then this indicates that the sitter has plans for a new venture, path or phase in their life. However, at the moment, these plans are at the back of the sitter's mind. These plans are something that the sitter is considering putting into action in the near future, as they are still working on them, costing them out or carrying out research.

07 The Chariot

Angel Wings

Symbolises protection, affection, hope and happiness.

Within a reading, a pair of Angel wings on their own simply represents that some aspect of the sitter's life is going well. Even if they are unhappy with recent developments, they should be encouraged to concentrate on the good things that have happened and that are still going on around them.

Arch

Symbolises new beginnings.

Within a reading, the arch suggests that the sitter is about to take a new direction in life – whether they know it or not. A new opportunity is about to present itself to the sitter. This could be a new opening at work, a new career path for them to follow or possibly a new romantic involvement.

Armour

Symbolises protection and strength.

Within a reading, the appearance of armour suggests that the sitter is feeling vulnerable in some way and that they feel the need to protect themselves from their perceived threat.

Baton

Symbolises spiritual authority or the development of ideas.

Within a reading, the baton represents the need of the sitter to take control of some aspect of the life, to be more authoritative in their dealings with others.

Castle

Symbolises goals and achievements.

Within a reading, a castle represents the sitter's long and difficult journey to achieve their goal in life. This might be a long university degree course, or a long battle against illness. Whatever the sitter's goal is, they are well on their way to achieving it. On a simpler note, a castle can represent security or sanctuary.

City / Village

Symbolises protection, harmony and teamwork.

Within a reading, a city, town or village appearing in the spread represents a place where people gather. Whatever the sitter is trying to do in life, they cannot do it alone. A group effort is required and the sitter should try and find the group that they need in order to accomplish their goals.

Horse

Symbolises strength and freedom.

Within a reading, a horse refers to the sitter's personal drive and a desire to free themselves from the current path that they are following. The sitter has the strength and stamina to easily achieve this goal, but they have to believe in themselves. Horses are also regarded as a deep spiritual sign, which might hint at the sitter's need for some spiritual guidance. Maybe the sitter needs to free themselves from old beliefs.

Moon

Symbolises cycles.

Within a reading, the appearance of the moon in a spread indicates that the sitter is moving from one phase of their life to another. Whatever transition is taking place in the sitter's life, it is for the sitter's overall good and/or wellbeing. The moon can also indicate that the sitter is quite a spiritual person, who might very well be starting to realise that they have psychic abilities themselves.

Sphinx

Symbolises mystery.

Within a reading, the ancient Sphinx represents the keeper of secrets and the mysteries of life. For the sitter this implies that they are trying to solve a riddle or mystery in their life. This usually consists of some information that has come their way, which is causing them some confusion. The sitter will have to dig deep and/or carry out some research in order to solve this mystery.

Star (Stars)

Symbolises guidance.

Within a reading, the appearance of stars in the spread indicates that the sitter is experiencing some turmoil in their life at the moment. Their life seems to be a little topsy-turvy right now, causing them a lot of confusion. The star symbol deals with shedding some light into their life. They must focus on one problem at a time and deal with it, moving onto the next problem and dealing with that and so on. There is light at the end of the tunnel, but the illumination of that light comes from within.

Yin Yang

Symbolises balance.

Within a reading, the appearance of the yin-yang symbol can be interpreted in different ways. The surrounding cards will indicate which interpretation applies to the sitter. It infers that the sitter is trying to achieve some balance in their life, or that possibly they have recently achieved the balance that they seek. This symbol can also imply that the sitter is being drawn in two different directions by some seemingly opposite or contrary forces that might actually be complementary and interconnected. The old saying of ‘opposites attract’ springs to mind.

08 Strength

Arch

Symbolises new beginnings.

Within a reading, the arch suggests that the sitter is about to take a new direction in life – whether they know it or not. A new opportunity is about to present itself to the sitter. This could be a new opening at work, a new career path for them to follow or possibly a new romantic involvement.

Infinity Symbol

Symbolises endless possibilities.

Within a reading, the Infinity Symbol (The Lemniscate) represents the never-ending possibilities in our lives. For the sitter, it implies that they possess the necessary endless energy to face whatever life throws at them. It can also represent everlasting love.

Lion

Symbolises courage and strength.

Within a reading, a lion can indicate that the sitter has the necessary personal courage and emotional strength required to overcome the difficulties that they are facing right now. Just as the lion is fearless, it is time for the sitter to conquer his or her own fears. Fear can hold us back, so conquering your fears will is the key to the sitter achieving the success that they desire.

Mountains

Symbolises challenges.

Within a reading, mountains usually appear in the background of the card. For the sitter, this suggests that they are facing seemingly insurmountable challenges, but that the sitter is trying to ignore them, pushing them to the back of their mind. If mountains appear in the majority of the spread, this indicates that the time has come for the sitter to face those challenges and to deal with them.

Pillar

Symbolises stability.

Within a reading, a pillar or pillars, represent strength, stability and balance. A single pillar can suggest that the sitter is the one who is supporting those around them, as in 'a pillar of strength’. When two pillars appear, usually at each side of the card, this could indicate that the sitter should consider their problems in a more diplomatic, or balanced way. Rather than left or right or black and white, the sitter should try to consider a more central view. In other words, the sitter should adopt a new perspective, a middle-of-the-road approach when tackling their problems.

Roses

Symbolises balance.

Within a reading, a rose, or roses, have always been associated with love, affection and relationships. For the sitter, they should remember that the rose represents promise and new beginnings. However, the sitter should be aware of the fact that the rose also has thorns. The thorns can represent possible painful ordeals along the way. As beautiful as a rose is, there is a balance to be struck.

09 The Hermit

Hood

Symbolises protection.

Within a reading, a hood represents that the sitter feels the need to protect themselves from someone or something. It can also suggest that the sitter is trying to hide something from someone, or possibly that someone is trying to hide something from the sitter. Lastly, it can imply that the sitter really needs to shut themselves away from others for a while, just to have some alone time.

Ice

Symbolises difficult territory.

Within a reading, ice usually appears on mountaintops in the background of a card. This suggests that the sitter knows within themselves (at the back of their minds) that they need to calm down (cool it) and react less to a negative situation that they are facing.

Lantern (Lamp)

Symbolises finding your way.

Within a reading, a lantern (or lamp) indicates that the sitter might be struggling with life at the moment and could be feeling confused about their circumstances. Mentally, the sitter needs to use the lantern to light their way and find their true path in life.

Mountains

Symbolises challenges.

Within a reading, mountains usually appear in the background of the card. For the sitter, this suggests that they are facing seemingly insurmountable challenges, but that the sitter is trying to ignore them, pushing them to the back of their mind. If mountains appear in the majority of the spread, this indicates that the time has come for the sitter to face those challenges and to deal with them.

10 The Wheel of Fortune

Angels

Symbolises divine messengers.

Within a reading, the appearance of an Angel in the spread represents that some kind of important information is coming the sitter's way. This could manifest itself in some sort of inspirational way, or even in a 'light bulb' moment. However the sitter receives this important information, they must not ignore it.

Angel Wings

Symbolises protection, affection, hope and happiness.

Within a reading, a pair of Angel wings on their own simply represents that some aspect of the sitter's life is going well. Even if they are unhappy with recent developments, they should be encouraged to concentrate on the good things that have happened and that are still going on around them.

Bird

Any species of bird symbolises rising above the normal.

Within a reading, a bird represents the sitter's need to lighten their thoughts. To rise above the problems of the material world and to look at the bigger picture. A bird can also symbolise the sitter's need to look at and to raise their individual spirituality.

Bull

Symbolises power and stability.

Within a reading, the appearance of a bull can represent quite a few things for the sitter. It could point to the sitter's resistance to change, as in being 'bull headed'. However, it can also suggest to the sitter that the time has come to stand their ground and fight for what they believe in.

Clouds

Symbolises transition.

Within a reading, clouds have different meanings depending on what colour they are. In the suit of Swords, most of the clouds are dark and fast moving, representing that the sitter is probably going through a troublesome (or stormy) period in their life. However, dark clouds like these can also represent confusion, or clouded judgement.

Eagle

Symbolises a connection to spiritual powers, Spirit Guides and Teachers.

Within a reading, the appearance of an eagle is a really good sign for any sitter who is trying to develop their psychic ability. It represents the fact that the sitter is doing well in their studies and that they will soon rise to the elevated heights that they are trying to achieve.

Lion

Symbolises courage and strength.

Within a reading, a lion can indicate that the sitter has the necessary personal courage and emotional strength required to overcome the difficulties that they are facing right now. Just as the lion is fearless, it is time for the sitter to conquer his or her own fears. Fear can hold us back, so conquering your fears will is the key to the sitter achieving the success that they desire.

Mountains

Symbolises challenges.

Within a reading, mountains usually appear in the background of the card. For the sitter, this suggests that they are facing seemingly insurmountable challenges, but that the sitter is trying to ignore them, pushing them to the back of their mind. If mountains appear in the majority of the spread, this indicates that the time has come for the sitter to face those challenges and to deal with them.

Snake

Symbolises transformation.

Within a reading, a snake can symbolise renewal and rebirth, because it sheds its skin and re-emerges ready for its next phase in life. For the sitter, this can indicate that they should probably ask themselves if they need to 'shed' some part of themselves. Shedding some negative aspect of their life will allow them to grow and move on. A snake can also represent the fact that the sitter should be on the alert for so-called friends who really do not have their best interests at heart, a 'snake in the grass' so to speak.

Sphinx

Symbolises mystery.

Within a reading, the ancient Sphinx represents the keeper of secrets and the mysteries of life. For the sitter this implies that they are trying to solve a riddle or mystery in their life. This usually consists of some information that has come their way, which is causing them some confusion. The sitter will have to dig deep and/or carry out some research in order to solve this mystery.

Trees

Symbolises growth.

Within a reading, trees appear in many of the Tarot Cards, but significantly, they usually appear in the background. If trees appear in a lot of the cards within a spread, then this indicates that the sitter has plans for a new venture, path or phase in their life. However, at the moment, these plans are at the back of the sitter's mind. These plans are something that the sitter is considering putting into action in the near future, as they are still working on them, costing them out or carrying out research.

Wheel

Symbolises cycles.

Within a reading, a wheel represents different things depending on the surrounding cards. It can refer to the cycle of life, so possibly the sitter has recently experienced a birth and a death within their family group. It can also infer that the sitter is caught in a cycle of events that is causing them some difficulty and that they are really trying very hard to break free from that cycle. Lastly, it can represent that the sitter feels stuck in a repetitive cycle of work and sleep, and that they are trying to figure out a new path for themselves – possibly a new hobby for example.

Wolf

Symbolises loyalty.

Within a reading, the appearance of a wolf can indicate that the sitter's loyalties are being tested in some way. This could be a situation that has arisen at work, or within the sitter's circle of family and friends. The loyal and intelligent wolf reminds us that we do not have to 'follow the pack' or to try and 'fit in'. The sitter must be true to themselves and follow their heart when deciding where their loyalties lie.

Zodiac Circle

Symbolises our circle of friends.

Within a reading, the appearance of the zodiac circle comes as a reminder that we do not live our lives alone. We are surrounded by people from the other star signs and we are influenced by the character of the animals that some of them represent. For the sitter, if they are struggling a little at the moment, then they should turn to their ‘circle’ of family and friends for help, just as they would turn to the sitter in their hour of need if they had to.

11 Justice

Crown

Symbolises authority and power.

Within a reading, the appearance of a crown can signify many things. It could suggest that the sitter needs authority in their life. Possibly that the sitter desires recognition for their achievements. Or even that the sitter desires more control of their life, which might feel a little out of control to them at the moment.

Helmet

Symbolises protection.

Within a reading, a helmet can suggest that the sitter is feeling vulnerable in some way and is looking for a way to protect themselves from the cause. Usually a helmet has a plume or crest on top of it for identification. This could suggest that the sitter is searching for acceptance in some way.

Pillar

Symbolises stability.

Within a reading, a pillar or pillars, represent strength, stability and balance. A single pillar can suggest that the sitter is the one who is supporting those around them, as in 'a pillar of strength'. When two pillars appear, usually at each side of the card, this could indicate that the sitter should consider their problems in a more diplomatic, or balanced way. Rather than left or right or black and white, the sitter should try to consider a more central view. In other words, the sitter should adopt a new perspective, a middle-of-the-road approach when tackling their problems.

Scales

Symbolises balance.

Within a reading, scales have the fairly obvious meaning of balance. For the sitter however, the scales can represent that some aspect of their life is actually out of balance. Something in their life is throwing them out of kilter, so the sitter needs to identify the cause of this imbalance and take the required action in order to restore the equilibrium.

Scroll

Symbolises learning.

Within a reading, the appearance of a scroll indicates that the sitter has achieved something recently. This could be an educational achievement or possibly a goal in life. In certain cases, a scroll can indicate that the sitter is unaware of something that is coming their way. In this case, the scroll indicates that the sitter needs to learn something, to educate themselves about this impending situation in order for them to be able to deal with it properly.

Sword

Symbolises defending oneself.

Within a reading, the interpretation of a sword symbol is as two-edged as the sword itself. On one hand, the sword can indicate that the sitter feels threatened in some way. Whether at work or within the sitter's personal life, they feel the need to fight back or to defend themselves. On the other hand, a sword can also indicate that it is the sitter who is the aggressor. They might be forcing their view or opinion on others, upsetting them and making them feel they must defend themselves against the sitter.

(Note – this interpretation cannot be used for any card from the Suit of Swords in general, unless more than two cards from that suit appear in the spread.)

Throne

Symbolises stability.

Within a reading, as a throne is a seat of authority, this represents a position of responsibility for the sitter. Some aspect of the sitter's life is completely under their control. This could be a position at work, as in a managerial post. Possibly at home where the sitter has sole responsibility for raising a child or caring for someone for example. Whichever aspect of the sitter's life the throne refers to, it is running smoothly, but only because of the sitter's determination and steady hand.

Yin Yang

Symbolises balance.

Within a reading, the appearance of the yin-yang symbol can be interpreted in different ways. The surrounding cards will indicate which interpretation applies to the sitter. It infers that the sitter is trying to achieve some balance in their life, or that possibly they have recently achieved the balance that they seek. This symbol can also imply that the sitter is being drawn in two different directions by some seemingly opposite or contrary forces that might actually be complementary and interconnected. The old saying of 'opposites attract' springs to mind.

12 The Hanged Man

Hourglass

Symbolises the passage of time.

Within a reading, the appearance of an hourglass refers to the fact that the sitter is running out of time. The sitter has something that is blocking their progress and they must deal with it as soon as possible. They need to do what needs to be done in order to get on with their life.

Moon

Symbolises cycles.

Within a reading, the appearance of the moon in a spread indicates that the sitter is moving from one phase of their life to another. Whatever transition is taking place in the sitter's life, it is for the sitter's overall good and/or wellbeing. The moon can also indicate that the sitter is quite a spiritual person, who might very well be starting to realise that they have psychic abilities themselves.

Pillar

Symbolises stability.

Within a reading, a pillar or pillars, represent strength, stability and balance. A single pillar can suggest that the sitter is the one who is supporting those around them, as in 'a pillar of strength'. When two pillars appear, usually at each side of the card, this could indicate that the sitter should consider their problems in a more diplomatic, or balanced way. Rather than left or right or black and white, the sitter should try to consider a more central view. In other words, the sitter should adopt a new perspective, a middle-of-the-road approach when tackling their problems.

Ropes (Restraints)

Symbolises restriction.

Within a reading, the appearance of ropes, especially if being used to restrain someone, infers that the sitter is feeling restricted in some way. They might be experiencing a feeling of being trapped or helpless in their present situation. The sitter needs to relax, as the harder that they struggle against these symbolic ropes, the tighter they will become.

Trees

Symbolises growth.

Within a reading, trees appear in many of the Tarot Cards, but significantly, they usually appear in the background. If trees appear in a lot of the cards within a spread, then this indicates that the sitter has plans for a new venture, path or phase in their life. However, at the moment, these plans are at the back of the sitter's mind. These plans are something that the sitter is considering putting into action in the near future, as they are still working on them, costing them out or carrying out research.

13 Death

Armour

Symbolises protection and strength.

Within a reading, the appearance of armour suggests that the sitter is feeling vulnerable in some way and that they feel the need to protect themselves from their perceived threat.

Banner (Flag)

Symbolises a big transformation.

Within a reading, a flag or banner is an announcement of change in the sitter's life and the flag is telling the world all about it. However, it can also represent a rallying call, asking people (probably family) to rally around the sitter's new cause.

Crown

Symbolises authority and power.

Within a reading, the appearance of a crown can signify many things. It could suggest that the sitter needs authority in their life. Possibly that the sitter desires recognition for their achievements. Or even that the sitter desires more control of their life, which might feel a little out of control to them at the moment.

Horse

Symbolises strength and freedom.

Within a reading, a horse refers to the sitter's personal drive and a desire to free themselves from the current path that they are following. The sitter has the strength and stamina to easily achieve this goal, but they have to believe in themselves. Horses are also regarded as a deep spiritual sign, which might hint at the sitter's need for some spiritual guidance. Maybe the sitter needs to free themselves from old beliefs.

Pillar

Symbolises stability.

Within a reading, a pillar or pillars, represent strength, stability and balance. A single pillar can suggest that the sitter is the one who is supporting those around them, as in 'a pillar of strength'. When two pillars appear, usually at each side of the card, this could indicate that the sitter should consider their problems in a more diplomatic, or balanced way. Rather than left or right or black and white, the sitter should try to consider a more central view. In other words, the sitter should adopt a new perspective, a middle-of-the-road approach when tackling their problems.

Roses

Symbolises balance.

Within a reading, a rose, or roses, have always been associated with love, affection and relationships. For the sitter, they should remember that the rose represents promise and new beginnings. However, the sitter should be aware of the fact that the rose also has thorns. The thorns can represent possible painful ordeals along the way. As beautiful as a rose is, there is a balance to be struck.

Scorpion

Symbolises potential threats.

Within a reading, a scorpion is a strong spiritual sign that represents self-defence or protection. In a spread, it infers that the sitter needs to protect themselves from possible attack, guarding their flank and keep an eye on their blind spots. This is not a warning about physical attack, this is more in the area of an emotional attack or possibly slander. Keeping themselves aware in this way will protect the sitter from potential threats.

Skeleton (or Skull)

Symbolises transition.

Within a reading, while most of us look upon skulls and skeletons as a creepy reminder of our own mortality, they have a completely different meaning in the Tarot. For the sitter, a skull or a skeleton represents half-formed, or not fully developed ideas or plans. The sitter might be in the early stages of their project, but they can take comfort with the appearance of skulls or skeletons, as they represent change, transition or transformation, usually for the better.

Spider

Symbolises resilience.

Within a reading, the industrious spider will build and rebuild its web, no matter how many times it is destroyed by the elements. For the sitter this can represent that they are trying to achieve a goal in their life, but that they are constantly being knocked back or blocked in some way. No matter what, in order to achieve their goal, the sitter must never give up. Try, try and try again – they will get there in the end.

Sun

Symbolises life and rebirth.

Within a reading, just as the sun rises every morning, so a new day begins for the sitter. The position of the sun in a Tarot card is also significant. A rising sun promises new beginnings, while a setting sun infers that something is coming to an end. A full mid-day sun indicates energy, strength and success in creative endeavours.

14 Temperance

Angels

Symbolises divine messengers.

Within a reading, the appearance of an Angel in the spread represents that some kind of important information is coming the sitter's way. This could manifest itself in some sort of inspirational way, or even in a 'light bulb' moment. However the sitter receives this important information, they must not ignore it.

Angel Wings

Symbolises protection, affection, hope and happiness.

Within a reading, a pair of Angel wings on their own simply represents that some aspect of the sitter's life is going well. Even if they are unhappy with recent developments, they should be encouraged to concentrate on the good things that have happened and that are still going on around them.

Fire (Flames)

Symbolises transformation.

Within a reading, fire or flames represents that the sitter is going through some kind of transition in their life. They can also represent that the sitter might need to make some kind of change, alteration or modification to their lifestyle.

Goblet/Chalice

Symbolises family and tradition.

Within a reading, the appearance of a goblet or chalice indicates that family is extremely important to the sitter. It implies that the sitter probably possesses a pretty traditional view of what family life means to them. In particular, children and grandchildren mean everything to them and are their very reason for being.

Hills

Symbolises obstacles.

Within a reading, the appearance of hills in the spread suggests that the sitter is facing obstacles in their life that they need to overcome. However daunting or impossible these hurdles might appear to be for the sitter, they need to remove these obstacles in their life in order to move on.

Lilies

Symbolises purity, love and relationships.

Within a reading, the appearance of a lily, or lilies, refers to a period of personal growth and development for the sitter. The lily can also indicate that the sitter (or someone that they are close to) is about to embark on a new relationship or that there is a birth in their immediate future.

Path (Road)

Symbolises life choices.

Within a reading, a path or a road refers to the fact that the sitter is facing a new path in life. The sitter might be about to set out on that new path, or may already have taken their first few steps on it. Either way, this path represents a whole new and potentially exciting future for the sitter. If they are having any doubts about this new path, they shouldn't worry, as it will be the right choice for them.

River

Symbolises obstacles.

Within a reading, the appearance of a river can be interpreted in two different ways. For the sitter, a river can represent an obstacle that they have to get across, as it is blocking their path or progress. On the other hand, it could be advising the sitter to stop struggling with whatever problem that they are facing or dealing with. It is time for them to 'go with the flow' and let the problem resolve itself.

Stained Glass

Symbolises your outlook.

Within a reading, when stained glass appears in the spread, it is often regarded as the spiritual window to the soul. For the sitter however, it is a sign that the time has come to start being honest with themselves about a situation that is unfolding around them. They must ask themselves if they are looking at this situation clearly, or are they looking at it through 'rose coloured glasses'?

Sun

Symbolises life and rebirth.

Within a reading, just as the sun rises every morning, so a new day begins for the sitter. The position of the sun in a Tarot card is also significant. A rising sun promises new beginnings, while a setting sun infers that something is coming to an end. A full mid-day sun indicates energy, strength and success in creative endeavours.

Triangle

Symbolises strength.

Within a reading, the triangle is the strongest basic geometric shape known to man, which is why it is used to support a roof in a domestic building for example. It is this very strength of the triangle which is significant in a reading. It infers that the sitter has a strong character, as in moral strength rather than physical strength. Whatever life throws at this particular sitter, they can handle it.

Water

Symbolises cleansing.

Within a reading, water usually represents the need for the sitter to 'cleanse' themselves. Not in the physical sense of needing a wash, but in an emotional or spiritual sense. In other words, the sitter needs to 'wash away' whatever it is that is troubling them. This would normally be an old memory, experience or episode in their life that is holding the sitter back. Once they have removed the issues that are bothering them, they will feel reborn and ready to move on with their life.

15 The Devil

Altar

Symbolises a sacred place.

Within a reading, an altar implies that the sitter is in need of some personal space within their busy life. They need this personal space in order to have some time to themselves, maybe to pursue their interest in a hobby, or more importantly, to develop their individual spirituality.

Chains

Symbolises restraint or restriction.

Within a reading, chains represent that the sitter is feeling held back, or being prevented from carrying out some action or other. If the chains are presented as some form of jewellery, then the sitter's problem is of a more delicate nature.

Devil

Symbolises materialism.

Within a reading, the appearance of the Devil represents that the sitter is probably more concerned with the material world and all of the pleasures that it can bring. It is really time for the sitter to start looking beyond the material world and look within themselves to discover what is really important in life.

Fire (Flames)

Symbolises transformation.

Within a reading, fire or flames represents that the sitter is going through some kind of transition in their life. They can also represent that the sitter might need to make some kind of change, alteration or modification to their lifestyle.

Horns

Symbolises physical prowess.

Within a reading, the appearance of horns indicates that the sitter is experiencing (or is in need of) fighting spirit in order to overcome a challenge that they are currently facing. It can also infer that the sitter has to take this challenge head on (by the horns), as there is really no other way of dealing with it.

Hourglass

Symbolises the passage of time.

Within a reading, the appearance of an hourglass refers to the fact that the sitter is running out of time. The sitter has something that is blocking their progress and they must deal with it as soon as possible. They need to do what needs to be done in order to get on with their life.

Pentangle

Symbolises the five senses

Within a reading, the Devil card represents materialism. The appearance of a pentangle on this card can indicate that the sitter is too concerned with the materialistic side of life and not paying enough attention to their spiritual self. The pentangle can also represent the five virtues, which are generosity, fellowship, chastity, courtesy and charity. The sitter should consider trying to follow one of these paths to start their journey away from materialism.

Pillar

Symbolises stability.

Within a reading, a pillar or pillars, represent strength, stability and balance. A single pillar can suggest that the sitter is the one who is supporting those around them, as in 'a pillar of strength'. When two pillars appear, usually at each side of the card, this could indicate that the sitter should consider their problems in a more diplomatic, or balanced way. Rather than left or right or black and white, the sitter should try to consider a more central view. In other words, the sitter should adopt a new perspective, a middle-of-the-road approach when tackling their problems.

16 The Tower

Clouds

Symbolises transition.

Within a reading, clouds have different meanings depending on what colour they are. In the suit of Swords, most of the clouds are dark and fast moving, representing that the sitter is probably going through a troublesome (or stormy) period in their life. However, dark clouds like these can also represent confusion, or clouded judgement.

Crown

Symbolises authority and power.

Within a reading, the appearance of a crown can signify many things. It could suggest that the sitter needs authority in their life. Possibly that the sitter desires recognition for their achievements. Or even that the sitter desires more control of their life, which might feel a little out of control to them at the moment.

Falling Man

Symbolises a fall from grace.

Within a reading, the image of the falling man indicates that the sitter is feeling in a precarious position at present. Whether relating to a relationship or work situation, the sitter feels that they are walking a tightrope and could slip at any moment.

Fire (Flames)

Symbolises transformation.

Within a reading, fire or flames represents that the sitter is going through some kind of transition in their life. They can also represent that the sitter might need to make some kind of change, alteration or modification to their lifestyle.

Ice

Symbolises difficult territory.

Within a reading, ice usually appears on mountaintops in the background of a card. This suggests that the sitter knows within themselves (at the back of their minds) that they need to calm down (cool it) and react less to a negative situation that they are facing.

Lightening

Symbolises a destructive force.

Within a reading, lightening suggests that the sitter must start to pay attention to their surroundings. It indicates that there is a destructive or disruptive force at work in their life. The sitter must identify that force (or indeed the person behind it) and stop it before it causes any more damage.

Moon

Symbolises cycles.

Within a reading, the appearance of the moon in a spread indicates that the sitter is moving from one phase of their life to another. Whatever transition is taking place in the sitter's life, it is for the sitter's overall good and/or wellbeing. The moon can also indicate that the sitter is quite a spiritual person, who might very well be starting to realise that they have psychic abilities themselves.

Tower

Symbolises sanctuary.

Within a reading, a tower represents sanctuary, a safe place that we can retreat to when things get too much for us. This safe place can simply be within our own minds, possibly just reliving old memories that bring us a degree of comfort. Anybody can take their mind away from the pressures of life by daydreaming for example. On the other hand, the tower can represent an actual physical location where the sitter feels safe and relaxed, usually their own home. In the Tower Card, the tower is being damaged by lightening. This can imply that the sitter's 'safe place' is under threat in some way.

Trees

Symbolises growth.

Within a reading, trees appear in many of the Tarot Cards, but significantly, they usually appear in the background. If trees appear in a lot of the cards within a spread, then this indicates that the sitter has plans for a new venture, path or phase in their life. However, at the moment, these plans are at the back of the sitter's mind. These plans are something that the sitter is considering putting into action in the near future, as they are still working on them, costing them out or carrying out research.

17 The Star

Bird

Any species of bird symbolises rising above the normal.

Within a reading, a bird represents the sitter's need to lighten their thoughts. To rise above the problems of the material world and to look at the bigger picture. A bird can also symbolise the sitter's need to look at and to raise their individual spirituality.

Dove

Symbolises peace, purity and love.

Within a reading, a dove can represent many things. It is a symbol of peace and love, but it is also regarded by many as a true spiritual sign. If the sitter has been experiencing a troubling time recently, the dove can be regarded as a sign that their troubles will soon be over and that peace and tranquillity will soon be restored.

Pitcher

Symbolises what lies within.

Within a reading, a pitcher (or jug) is a vessel or a container. What is of interest to us, is what is in the pitcher. It is exactly the same principle for the sitter. The sitter needs to re-examine themselves and decide what kind of vessel are they? What type of contents fill their heart or soul? It should be pure, but if it is not – then why not? Is there anything that they can do to improve their spiritual core?

Star (Stars)

Symbolises guidance.

Within a reading, the appearance of stars in the spread indicates that the sitter is experiencing some turmoil in their life at the moment. Their life seems to be a little topsy-turvy right now, causing them a lot of confusion. The star symbol deals with shedding some light into their life. They must focus on one problem at a time and deal with it, moving onto the next problem and dealing with that and so on. There is light at the end of the tunnel, but the illumination of that light comes from within.

Trees

Symbolises growth.

Within a reading, trees appear in many of the Tarot Cards, but significantly, they usually appear in the background. If trees appear in a lot of the cards within a spread, then this indicates that the sitter has plans for a new venture, path or phase in their life. However, at the moment, these plans are at the back of the sitter's mind. These plans are something that the sitter is considering putting into action in the near future, as they are still working on them, costing them out or carrying out research.

Water

Symbolises cleansing.

Within a reading, water usually represents the need for the sitter to 'cleanse' themselves. Not in the physical sense of needing a wash, but in an emotional or spiritual sense. In other words, the sitter needs to 'wash away' whatever it is that is troubling them. This would normally be an old memory, experience or episode in their life that is holding the sitter back. Once they have removed the issues that are bothering them, they will feel reborn and ready to move on with their life.

18 The Moon

Dog/Dogs

Symbolises loyalty or devotion.

Within a reading, whenever a dog (or dogs) appear in the spread it represents that the sitter might be experiencing loyalty issues. However, a dog can also represent that the sitter is on the right track in life, as dogs are symbolic of stability and steadfastness.

Lobster

Symbolises hidden psychic ability.

Within a reading, a lobster (or a crab or crayfish) is a reminder to the sitter that they should try and lose their hard outer protective shell and allow their visionary inner self to come out and develop. Those 'gut feelings' that the sitter is experiencing are actually a strong psychic talent that they possess and that it is time to set it free.

Moon

Symbolises cycles.

Within a reading, the appearance of the moon in a spread indicates that the sitter is moving from one phase of their life to another. Whatever transition is taking place in the sitter's life, it is for the sitter's overall good and/or wellbeing. The moon can also indicate that the sitter is quite a spiritual person, who might very well be starting to realise that they have psychic abilities themselves.

Path (Road)

Symbolises life choices.

Within a reading, a path or a road refers to the fact that the sitter is facing a new path in life. The sitter might be about to set out on that new path, or may already have taken their first few steps on it. Either way, this path represents a whole new and potentially exciting future for the sitter. If they are having any doubts about this new path, they shouldn't worry, as it will be the right choice for them.

Pillar
Symbolises stability.

Within a reading, a pillar or pillars, represent strength, stability and balance. A single pillar can suggest that the sitter is the one who is supporting those around them, as in 'a pillar of strength'. When two pillars appear, usually at each side of the card, this could indicate that the sitter should consider their problems in a more diplomatic, or balanced way. Rather than left or right or black and white, the sitter should try to consider a more central view. In other words, the sitter should adopt a new perspective, a middle-of-the-road approach when tackling their problems.

Rain
Symbolises renewal and regeneration.

Within a reading, rain is traditionally regarded as a sign of cleansing. For the sitter, this can be interpreted as a need to 'wash' away the old in order to embrace the new. Whatever is weighing down the sitter emotionally, now is the time to unburden themselves with the problems of the past and turn their heart to the future.

Reeds
Symbolises versatility.

Within a reading, the appearance of reeds indicates that the sitter might be experiencing confusion in their life. The rapidly growing, very adaptable and flexible reed, is a reminder to the sitter to rise above it all. Although the sitter's mind might be reeling with all the confusion that surrounds them at the moment, now is the time to rise above their conflicting emotions and see the bigger picture. The sitter needs a broader perspective in order to make sense of the confusion.

Tower
Symbolises sanctuary.

Within a reading, a tower represents sanctuary, a safe place that we can retreat to when things get too much for us. This safe place can simply be within our own minds, possibly just reliving old memories that bring us a degree of comfort. Anybody can take their mind away from the pressures of life by daydreaming for example. On the other hand, the tower can represent an actual physical location where the sitter feels safe and relaxed, usually their own home. In the Tower Card, the tower is being damaged by lightening. This can imply that the sitter's 'safe place' is under threat in some way.

Water

Symbolises cleansing.

Within a reading, water usually represents the need for the sitter to 'cleanse' themselves. Not in the physical sense of needing a wash, but in an emotional or spiritual sense. In other words, the sitter needs to 'wash away' whatever it is that is troubling them. This would normally be an old memory, experience or episode in their life that is holding the sitter back. Once they have removed the issues that are bothering them, they will feel reborn and ready to move on with their life.

Wolf

Symbolises loyalty.

Within a reading, the appearance of a wolf can indicate that the sitter's loyalties are being tested in some way. This could be a situation that has arisen at work, or within the sitter's circle of family and friends. The loyal and intelligent wolf reminds us that we do not have to 'follow the pack' or to try and 'fit in'. The sitter must be true to themselves and follow their heart when deciding where their loyalties lie.

19 The Sun

Banner (Flag)

Symbolises a big transformation.

Within a reading, a flag or banner is an announcement of change in the sitter's life and the flag is telling the world all about it. However, it can also represent a rallying call, asking people (probably family) to rally around the sitter's new cause.

Brick Wall

Symbolises a self-imposed barrier, or mental block.

Within a reading, a brick wall represents that the sitter is separating themselves from a problem, trying to shut that problem out of their mind. It is reluctance on the sitter's part to acknowledge what is happening around them. It can also represent the sitter holding themselves back or doubting themselves.

Child/Children

Symbolises innocence and memories.

Within a reading, a child or children appearing in the spread signifies that the sitter might be living in the past too much. Childhood memories can be happy or sad, but should never be dwelled upon. However, children in the tarot can also represent promise for the future, or the beginning of a new venture, as well as a child-like enthusiasm for life.

Horse

Symbolises strength and freedom.

Within a reading, a horse refers to the sitter's personal drive and a desire to free themselves from the current path that they are following. The sitter has the strength and stamina to easily achieve this goal, but they have to believe in themselves. Horses are also regarded as a deep spiritual sign, which might hint at the sitter's need for some spiritual guidance. Maybe the sitter needs to free themselves from old beliefs.

Orrery (model of the solar system)

Symbolises personal viewpoint.

Within a reading, the Orrery suggests that the sitter likes to be the centre of attention. However, this character trait can sometimes be misinterpreted as being a bit needy, so the sitter needs to be made aware of this fact. By contrast, it can also represent that the sitter enjoys being at the centre of things – in the thick of it.

Scales

Symbolises balance.

Within a reading, scales have the fairly obvious meaning of balance. For the sitter however, the scales can represent that some aspect of their life is actually out of balance. Something in their life is throwing them out of kilter, so the sitter needs to identify the cause of this imbalance and take the required action in order to restore the equilibrium.

Sun

Symbolises life and rebirth.

Within a reading, just as the sun rises every morning, so a new day begins for the sitter. The position of the sun in a Tarot card is also significant. A rising sun promises new beginnings, while a setting sun infers that something is coming to an end. A full mid-day sun indicates energy, strength and success in creative endeavours.

Sunflower

Symbolises positivity.

Within a reading, because sunflowers are such 'happy' flowers, they brighten up the lives of all who look at them. For the sitter however, it can imply that they are feeling a little down, in the doldrums so to speak. The sunflower is urging the sitter to stop looking at the dark side of their situation, as focusing on what is wrong in their life will only depress them more. They should start looking at the lighter side of life, as concentrating on the good or happy things in life will lift their mood.

Wall

Symbolises barriers.

Within a reading, a wall represents building a barrier in life. For the sitter, this refers to them needing to separate one area of their life from another. The surrounding cards should give an indication as to what areas need separating. It can also suggest that the sitter is holding back in some way, hiding behind a wall of their own making. However, a wall can also suggest quite simply that the sitter is in need of some privacy.

Yellow Flowers

Symbolises friendship.

Within a reading, any yellow flower is regarded as a symbol of the bonds of friendship that exist in our lives. For the sitter, apart from indicating friendship, yellow flowers can also be a sign that they have enjoyed some success recently. Lastly, the bright and sunny colour of a yellow flower can also indicate that the sitter is one of life's optimists, always seeing the good in people and events.

20 Judgement

Angels

Symbolises divine messengers.

Within a reading, the appearance of an Angel in the spread represents that some kind of important information is coming the sitter’s way. This could manifest itself in some sort of inspirational way, or even in a ‘light bulb’ moment. However the sitter receives this important information, they must not ignore it.

Angel Wings

Symbolises protection, affection, hope and happiness.

Within a reading, a pair of Angel wings on their own simply represents that some aspect of the sitter’s life is going well. Even if they are unhappy with recent developments, they should be encouraged to concentrate on the good things that have happened and that are still going on around them.

Banner (Flag)

Symbolises a big transformation.

Within a reading, a flag or banner is an announcement of change in the sitter’s life and the flag is telling the world all about it. However, it can also represent a rallying call, asking people (probably family) to rally around the sitter’s new cause.

Clouds

Symbolises transition.

Within a reading, clouds have different meanings depending on what colour they are. In the suit of Swords, most of the clouds are dark and fast moving, representing that the sitter is probably going through a troublesome (or stormy) period in their life. However, dark clouds like these can also represent confusion, or clouded judgement.

Hills

Symbolises obstacles.

Within a reading, the appearance of hills in the spread suggests that the sitter is facing obstacles in their life that they need to overcome. However daunting or impossible these hurdles might appear to be for the sitter, they need to remove these obstacles in their life in order to move on.

Ice

Symbolises difficult territory.

Within a reading, ice usually appears on mountaintops in the background of a card. This suggests that the sitter knows within themselves (at the back of their minds) that they need to calm down (cool it) and react less to a negative situation that they are facing.

Mountains

Symbolises challenges.

Within a reading, mountains usually appear in the background of the card. For the sitter, this suggests that they are facing seemingly insurmountable challenges, but that the sitter is trying to ignore them, pushing them to the back of their mind. If mountains appear in the majority of the spread, this indicates that the time has come for the sitter to face those challenges and to deal with them.

Tomb

Symbolises freeing yourself.

Within a reading, the appearance of a tomb never represents physical death. Instead, it indicates that the time has come for the sitter to 'lay to rest' any thoughts or memories that are troubling them. Freeing themselves from those troubling thoughts or memories will allow the sitter to escape from a period of mental stagnation. This will set them free to start a new phase of understanding that will improve their life.

Trumpet (Horn)

Symbolises announcement.

Within a reading, horns represent a joyous or triumphant period in the sitter's life. The sitter has something to shout about, something that they need to tell the world about – but not quite yet. They are waiting for the right time to make their happy announcement. Although filled with excitement, the sitter will know when the time is just right to announce their happy news of what has happened, or what it is that is about to happen.

Water

Symbolises cleansing.

Within a reading, water usually represents the need for the sitter to ‘cleanse’ themselves. Not in the physical sense of needing a wash, but in an emotional or spiritual sense. In other words, the sitter needs to ‘wash away’ whatever it is that is troubling them. This would normally be an old memory, experience or episode in their life that is holding the sitter back. Once they have removed the issues that are bothering them, they will feel reborn and ready to move on with their life.

21 The World

Baton

Symbolises spiritual authority or the development of ideas.

Within a reading, the baton represents the need of the sitter to take control of some aspect of the life, to be more authoritative in their dealings with others.

Bird

Any species of bird symbolises rising above the normal.

Within a reading, a bird represents the sitter's need to lighten their thoughts. To rise above the problems of the material world and to look at the bigger picture. A bird can also symbolise the sitter's need to look at and to raise their individual spirituality.

Bull

Symbolises power and stability.

Within a reading, the appearance of a bull can represent quite a few things for the sitter. It could point to the sitter's resistance to change, as in being 'bull headed'. However, it can also suggest to the sitter that the time has come to stand their ground and fight for what they believe in.

Clouds

Symbolises transition.

Within a reading, clouds have different meanings depending on what colour they are. In the suit of Swords, most of the clouds are dark and fast moving, representing that the sitter is probably going through a troublesome (or stormy) period in their life. However, dark clouds like these can also represent confusion, or clouded judgement.

Eagle

Symbolises a connection to spiritual powers, Spirit Guides and Teachers.

Within a reading, the appearance of an eagle is a really good sign for any sitter who is trying to develop their psychic ability. It represents the fact that the sitter is doing well in their studies and that they will soon rise to the elevated heights that they are trying to achieve.

Earth (The Planet)

Symbolises Nature (as in Mother Earth) fertility and life.

Within a reading, the appearance of planet Earth indicates that the sitter has a keen affinity with nature and the natural world. As the Earth is a sphere, this can also indicate that the sitter is currently experiencing completeness in some aspect of their life.

Hourglass

Symbolises the passage of time.

Within a reading, the appearance of an hourglass refers to the fact that the sitter is running out of time. The sitter has something that is blocking their progress and they must deal with it as soon as possible. They need to do what needs to be done in order to get on with their life.

Infinity Symbol

Symbolises endless possibilities.

Within a reading, the Infinity Symbol (The Lemniscate) represents the never-ending possibilities in our lives. For the sitter, it implies that they possess the necessary endless energy to face whatever life throws at them. It can also represent everlasting love.

Laurel Wreath

Symbolises achievement.

Within a reading, the appearance of a laurel wreath indicates that the sitter has recently achieved something in their life that they are very proud of. This could be anything from passing an exam, getting the job that they have always wanted or overcoming some personal problem that has been holding them back.

Lion

Symbolises courage and strength.

Within a reading, a lion can indicate that the sitter has the necessary personal courage and emotional strength required to overcome the difficulties that they are facing right now. Just as the lion is fearless, it is time for the sitter to conquer his or her own fears. Fear can hold us back, so conquering your fears will is the key to the sitter achieving the success that they desire.

Zodiac Circle

Symbolises our circle of friends.

Within a reading, the appearance of the zodiac circle comes as a reminder that we do not live our lives alone. We are surrounded by people from the other star signs and we are influenced by the character of the animals that some of them represent. For the sitter, if they are struggling a little at the moment, then they should turn to their 'circle' of family and friends for help, just as they would turn to the sitter in their hour of need if they had to.

22 The Ace of Swords

Amethyst

Symbolises healing.

Within a reading, an amethyst (or the colour purple) tells the reader that the sitter is in need of some kind of healing. This could be the sitter's emotional issues or possibly their physical ailments. More simply, purple could suggest that the sitter needs some aspect of their life 'healed'.

Clouds

Symbolises transition.

Within a reading, clouds have different meanings depending on what colour they are. In the suit of Swords, most of the clouds are dark and fast moving, representing that the sitter is probably going through a troublesome (or stormy) period in their life. However, dark clouds like these can also represent confusion, or clouded judgement.

Crown

Symbolises authority and power.

Within a reading, the appearance of a crown can signify many things. It could suggest that the sitter needs authority in their life. Possibly that the sitter desires recognition for their achievements. Or even that the sitter desires more control of their life, which might feel a little out of control to them at the moment.

Dark Skies (Storm Clouds)

Symbolises potential troubles.

Within a reading, the appearance of dark skies, or storm clouds, represents that the sitter is probably going through a rough patch in their life. On the other hand, dark skies, or stormy looking clouds, can also represent confusion about some issue in the sitter's life, or possibly that they are experiencing clouded judgement.

Eagle

Symbolises a connection to spiritual powers, Spirit Guides and Teachers.

Within a reading, the appearance of an eagle is a really good sign for any sitter who is trying to develop their psychic ability. It represents the fact that the sitter is doing well in their studies and that they will soon rise to the elevated heights that they are trying to achieve.

Hand

Symbolises transmission or give and take.

Within a reading, a hand or a pair of hands on their own implies that the sitter should understand that the problem that they are dealing with at this moment in their life, can only be solved with some kind of compromise. Hands give and receive, or give and take, so should the sitter.

Laurel Wreath

Symbolises achievement.

Within a reading, the appearance of a laurel wreath indicates that the sitter has recently achieved something in their life that they are very proud of. This could be anything from passing an exam, getting the job that they have always wanted or overcoming some personal problem that has been holding them back.

Triangle

Symbolises strength.

Within a reading, the triangle is the strongest basic geometric shape known to man, which is why it is used to support a roof in a domestic building for example. It is this very strength of the triangle which is significant in a reading. It infers that the sitter has a strong character, as in moral strength rather than physical strength. Whatever life throws at this particular sitter, they can handle it.

Zodiac Circle

Symbolises our circle of friends.

Within a reading, the appearance of the zodiac circle comes as a reminder that we do not live our lives alone. We are surrounded by people from the other star signs and we are influenced by the character of the animals that some of them represent. For the sitter, if they are struggling a little at the moment, then they should turn to their 'circle' of family and friends for help, just as they would turn to the sitter in their hour of need if they had to.

23 The Two of Swords

Bench

Symbolises the need to study the details.

Within a reading, a bench represents the need for the sitter to take their time and to examine the details of the situation that they currently find themselves in. Symbolically 'laying out the plans' and studying them.

Blindfold

Symbolises our inability to see things clearly.

Within a reading, a blindfold represents the sitter's unwillingness to face the truth about some troubling aspect of their life. Basically that the sitter is turning a blind eye. It can also be a sign that something is being kept, or hidden from them.

Chains

Symbolises restraint or restriction.

Within a reading, chains represent that the sitter is feeling held back, or being prevented from carrying out some action or other. If the chains are presented as some form of jewellery, then the sitter's problem is of a more delicate nature.

Moon

Symbolises cycles.

Within a reading, the appearance of the moon in a spread indicates that the sitter is moving from one phase of their life to another. Whatever transition is taking place in the sitter's life, it is for the sitter's overall good and/or wellbeing. The moon can also indicate that the sitter is quite a spiritual person, who might very well be starting to realise that they have psychic abilities themselves.

Sea (Ocean)

Symbolises an unsettled time.

Within a reading, the appearance of the sea is designed to make us think about our life. The sitter should consider the vastness and the strength of the sea. It can be calm, but it can suddenly turn violent and unleash its power. For the sitter this can indicate that their life has recently been full of ups and downs, as situations ebb and flow through their recent daily routine. They probably feel as if they have recently been washed about from pillar to post. Calm will return, but they will have to be patient and ride out the storm.

24 The Three of Swords

Clouds

Symbolises transition.

Within a reading, clouds have different meanings depending on what colour they are. In the suit of Swords, most of the clouds are dark and fast moving, representing that the sitter is probably going through a troublesome (or stormy) period in their life. However, dark clouds like these can also represent confusion, or clouded judgement.

Dark Skies (Storm Clouds)

Symbolises potential troubles.

Within a reading, the appearance of dark skies, or storm clouds, represents that the sitter is probably going through a rough patch in their life. On the other hand, dark skies, or stormy looking clouds, can also represent confusion about some issue in the sitter's life, or possibly that they are experiencing clouded judgement.

Heart

Symbolises love, joy and affection.

Within a reading, a heart suggests that the sitter needs to pay attention to the things that are important to them. The heart is also a symbol of truth, courage and loyalty. In that respect, it is probably time for the sitter to take stock of other people in their life, in order to see if these issues are reciprocated.

Rain

Symbolises renewal and regeneration.

Within a reading, rain is traditionally regarded as a sign of cleansing. For the sitter, this can be interpreted as a need to 'wash' away the old in order to embrace the new. Whatever is weighing down the sitter emotionally, now is the time to unburden themselves with the problems of the past and turn their heart to the future.

Teardrops

Symbolises sorrows.

Within a reading, the appearance of teardrops within a spread indicates that the sitter is going through a painful process of some description at the moment. This could be anything from the recent loss of a loved one, up to being plagued with painful memories of an incident from their past. It might take time, but the sitter will get over these sorrows. They can speed up the process if they can learn how to alter the way that they think.

25 The Four of Swords

Arch

Symbolises new beginnings.

Within a reading, the arch suggests that the sitter is about to take a new direction in life – whether they know it or not. A new opportunity is about to present itself to the sitter. This could be a new opening at work, a new career path for them to follow or possibly a new romantic involvement.

Armour

Symbolises protection and strength.

Within a reading, the appearance of armour suggests that the sitter is feeling vulnerable in some way and that they feel the need to protect themselves from their perceived threat.

Black Bird

Symbolises metaphorical death, as in something coming to an end.

Within a reading, the appearance of any species of black bird tells us that some aspect of the sitter's life is coming to an end. This could be a problem that they have been struggling with, or possibly a difficult phase in their life that they have been going through.

Pillar

Symbolises stability.

Within a reading, a pillar or pillars, represent strength, stability and balance. A single pillar can suggest that the sitter is the one who is supporting those around them, as in 'a pillar of strength'. When two pillars appear, usually at each side of the card, this could indicate that the sitter should consider their problems in a more diplomatic, or balanced way. Rather than left or right or black and white, the sitter should try to consider a more central view. In other words, the sitter should adopt a new perspective, a middle-of-the-road approach when tackling their problems.

Stained Glass

Symbolises your outlook.

Within a reading, when stained glass appears in the spread, it is often regarded as the spiritual window to the soul. For the sitter however, it is a sign that the time has come to start being honest with themselves about a situation that is unfolding around them. They must ask themselves if they are looking at this situation clearly, or are they looking at it through 'rose coloured glasses'?

Tomb

Symbolises freeing yourself.

Within a reading, the appearance of a tomb never represents physical death. Instead, it indicates that the time has come for the sitter to 'lay to rest' any thoughts or memories that are troubling them. Freeing themselves from those troubling thoughts or memories will allow the sitter to escape from a period of mental stagnation. This will set them free to start a new phase of understanding that will improve their life.

Window

Symbolises a new outlook.

Within a reading, a window represents a new perspective, or a new opportunity. However, it can also indicate that the sitter feels as if they are on the outside looking in. The time has come for the sitter to move inside and take an active part in whatever it is that they have been observing. Only by joining in will they be able to take advantage of all the new opportunities that will be within their grasp.

26 The Five of Swords

Armour

Symbolises protection and strength.

Within a reading, the appearance of armour suggests that the sitter is feeling vulnerable in some way and that they feel the need to protect themselves from their perceived threat.

Battle

Symbolises conflict or struggle.

Within a reading, a battle scene represents that the sitter is experiencing some kind of struggle in their life. This could be an emotional struggle, or possibly a struggle with a legal procedure.

Buckle (Silver)

Symbolises loyalty and trustworthiness.

Within a reading, a buckle can represent the sitter's need to 'buckle down' and get on with it. Whenever we use a buckle, we depend on it doing its job. In the same sense, a buckle can denote the sitter's sense of loyalty, trustworthiness and possibly even dependency.

Clouds

Symbolises transition.

Within a reading, clouds have different meanings depending on what colour they are. In the suit of Swords, most of the clouds are dark and fast moving, representing that the sitter is probably going through a troublesome (or stormy) period in their life. However, dark clouds like these can also represent confusion, or clouded judgement.

Dark Skies (Storm Clouds)

Symbolises potential troubles.

Within a reading, the appearance of dark skies, or storm clouds, represents that the sitter is probably going through a rough patch in their life. On the other hand, dark skies, or stormy looking clouds, can also represent confusion about some issue in the sitter's life, or possibly that they are experiencing clouded judgement.

Fire (Flames)

Symbolises transformation.

Within a reading, fire or flames represents that the sitter is going through some kind of transition in their life. They can also represent that the sitter might need to make some kind of change, alteration or modification to their lifestyle.

Gauntlets (Gloves)

Symbolises a challenge.

Within a reading, the appearance of a gauntlet represents that the sitter is facing some kind of challenge in their life, as in 'throwing down the gauntlet'. This could be a challenge that they face, or a challenge that they have made.

Sea (Ocean)

Symbolises an unsettled time.

Within a reading, the appearance of the sea is designed to make us think about our life. The sitter should consider the vastness and the strength of the sea. It can be calm, but it can suddenly turn violent and unleash its power. For the sitter this can indicate that their life has recently been full of ups and downs, as situations ebb and flow through their recent daily routine. They probably feel as if they have recently been washed about from pillar to post. Calm will return, but they will have to be patient and ride out the storm.

Shield

Symbolises protection.

Within a reading, the appearance of a shield represents that the sitter is in need of protecting themselves and those that they love from the harsh realities of life. No matter how happy, safe and secure they might feel at the moment, they should be deeply aware that they are as vulnerable as the rest of us. However, being aware of this vulnerability will allow them to prepare themselves in order to be ready to raise their protective shield whenever they need it.

Soldiers

Symbolises structure.

Within a reading, the appearance of a soldier or soldiers, indicates that the sitter is in need of some order in their life. Events are unfolding around them at a fast pace and everything seems chaotic to the sitter at the moment. They must discipline themselves to tackle each of their problems one by one, no matter what else is happening in the background. This is the only way that the sitter can sort out the chaos and bring structure back into their life.

Trees

Symbolises growth.

Within a reading, trees appear in many of the Tarot Cards, but significantly, they usually appear in the background. If trees appear in a lot of the cards within a spread, then this indicates that the sitter has plans for a new venture, path or phase in their life. However, at the moment, these plans are at the back of the sitter's mind. These plans are something that the sitter is considering putting into action in the near future, as they are still working on them, costing them out or carrying out research.

27 The Six of Swords

Arch

Symbolises new beginnings.

Within a reading, the arch suggests that the sitter is about to take a new direction in life – whether they know it or not. A new opportunity is about to present itself to the sitter. This could be a new opening at work, a new career path for them to follow or possibly a new romantic involvement.

Boat (Ship)

Symbolises moving away from past events.

Within a reading, any boat or ship that appears in the spread represents moving on for the sitter. This could signify moving away from emotional troubles. It can also represent that the sitter has, or is about to move onto a new path, or different direction in life.

Candelabra

Symbolises illuminating your way.

Within a reading, the appearance of a candelabra represents that the sitter needs to think carefully about which path in life they want to follow. Only by 'shining a light' on their chosen path will the sitter be able to navigate along that path, avoiding the obstacles.

Catacombs

Symbolises your deepest thoughts.

Within a reading, catacombs infer that the sitter is troubled with a series of unsettling thoughts from the darkest corners of their mind. However, it can also imply that the sitter is so lost in their deep thoughts that they are missing out on life.

Chains

Symbolises restraint or restriction.

Within a reading, chains represent that the sitter is feeling held back, or being prevented from carrying out some action or other. If the chains are presented as some form of jewellery, then the sitter's problem is of a more delicate nature.

Ferryman

Symbolises transition.

Within a reading, rivers or the Ferryman indicates that the sitter is at a threshold in life. It represents a crossing over from one path in life to another. However, some believe that the Ferryman can symbolise the presence of spirit guides or guardians.

Mountains

Symbolises challenges.

Within a reading, mountains usually appear in the background of the card. For the sitter, this suggests that they are facing seemingly insurmountable challenges, but that the sitter is trying to ignore them, pushing them to the back of their mind. If mountains appear in the majority of the spread, this indicates that the time has come for the sitter to face those challenges and to deal with them.

Paddle

Symbolises independence.

Within a reading, the appearance of a paddle is an indication to the sitter that the time has come to 'paddle your own canoe'. In other words, the time has come for the sitter to start acting independently and work towards deciding their own fate. The time has come to stop relying on, or listening to others.

Sea (Ocean)

Symbolises an unsettled time.

Within a reading, the appearance of the sea is designed to make us think about our life. The sitter should consider the vastness and the strength of the sea. It can be calm, but it can suddenly turn violent and unleash its power. For the sitter this can indicate that their life has recently been full of ups and downs, as situations ebb and flow through their recent daily routine. They probably feel as if they have recently been washed about from pillar to post. Calm will return, but they will have to be patient and ride out the storm.

Trees

Symbolises growth.

Within a reading, trees appear in many of the Tarot Cards, but significantly, they usually appear in the background. If trees appear in a lot of the cards within a spread, then this indicates that the sitter has plans for a new venture, path or phase in their life. However, at the moment, these plans are at the back of the sitter's mind. These plans are something that the sitter is considering putting into action in the near future, as they are still working on them, costing them out or carrying out research.

28 The Seven of Swords

Arm Band

Symbolises belonging.

Within a reading, an armband represents the need of the sitter to belong to something. This might be a group or organisation that the sitter feels attracted to.
(An armband can be a piece of material, a piece of jewellery or even a tattoo.)

Bird

Any species of bird symbolises rising above the normal.

Within a reading, a bird represents the sitter's need to lighten their thoughts. To rise above the problems of the material world and to look at the bigger picture. A bird can also symbolise the sitter's need to look at and to raise their individual spirituality.

Gauntlets (Gloves)

Symbolises a challenge.

Within a reading, the appearance of a gauntlet represents that the sitter is facing some kind of challenge in their life, as in 'throwing down the gauntlet'. This could be a challenge that they face, or a challenge that they have made.

Magpie

Symbolises balance in life.

Within a reading, a magpie can refer to the sitter's tendency to chase after false ideas or perceptions. Its appearance in the spread is a reminder to the sitter that the time has come to re-evaluate their priorities. The magpie's love of shiny or glittery things can suggest that the sitter could be more interested in the material side of life and ignoring their spiritual side.

Moon

Symbolises cycles.

Within a reading, the appearance of the moon in a spread indicates that the sitter is moving from one phase of their life to another. Whatever transition is taking place in the sitter's life, it is for the sitter's overall good and/or wellbeing. The moon can also indicate that the sitter is quite a spiritual person, who might very well be starting to realise that they have psychic abilities themselves.

Tents (Marquees)

Symbolises refuge.

Within a reading, a tent can represent a temporary refuge from the hustle and bustle of life. For the sitter it can indicate that life is starting to get them down and that they are looking for an escape. It should be pointed out that a tent is a temporary structure, which indicates that the difficulties that the sitter is experiencing right now are as temporary as the tent itself.

Window

Symbolises a new outlook.

Within a reading, a window represents a new perspective, or a new opportunity. However, it can also indicate that the sitter feels as if they are on the outside looking in. The time has come for the sitter to move inside and take an active part in whatever it is that they have been observing. Only by joining in will they be able to take advantage of all the new opportunities that will be within their grasp.

29 The Eight of Swords

Blindfold

Symbolises our inability to see things clearly.

Within a reading, a blindfold represents the sitter's unwillingness to face the truth about some troubling aspect of their life. Basically that the sitter is turning a blind eye. It can also be a sign that something is being kept, or hidden from them.

Castle

Symbolises goals and achievements.

Within a reading, a castle represents the sitter's long and difficult journey to achieve their goal in life. This might be a long university degree course, or a long battle against illness. Whatever the sitter's goal is, they are well on their way to achieving it. On a simpler note, a castle can represent security or sanctuary.

Cliff Edge

Signifies possible new opportunities.

Within a reading, a cliff edge can represent two things. The sitter is about to embark on a new path, which has been created by the arrival of a new opportunity in their life. On one hand, this is an exciting time for the sitter. On the other hand, they should take precautions, as there are potential pitfalls ahead.

Cobweb

Symbolises mystery, strength and growth.

Within a reading, the appearance of a cobweb represents that the choices that the sitter makes ultimately construct their life. We must 'weave' our lives as carefully and purposefully as the spider weaves his web.

Ropes (Restraints)

Symbolises restriction.

Within a reading, the appearance of ropes, especially if being used to restrain someone, infers that the sitter is feeling restricted in some way. They might be experiencing a feeling of being trapped or helpless in their present situation. The sitter needs to relax, as the harder that they struggle against these symbolic ropes, the tighter they will become.

Sea (Ocean)

Symbolises an unsettled time.

Within a reading, the appearance of the sea is designed to make us think about our life. The sitter should consider the vastness and the strength of the sea. It can be calm, but it can suddenly turn violent and unleash its power. For the sitter this can indicate that their life has recently been full of ups and downs, as situations ebb and flow through their recent daily routine. They probably feel as if they have recently been washed about from pillar to post. Calm will return, but they will have to be patient and ride out the storm.

Spider

Symbolises resilience.

Within a reading, the industrious spider will build and rebuild its web, no matter how many times it is destroyed by the elements. For the sitter this can represent that they are trying to achieve a goal in their life, but that they are constantly being knocked back or blocked in some way. No matter what, in order to achieve their goal, the sitter must never give up. Try, try and try again – they will get there in the end.

30 The Nine of Swords

Bed

Symbolises a retreat or a safe place.

Within a reading, a bed represents that the sitter might be feeling under pressure as a result of recent troubling events in their life. They need to sit down, relax and find some time for themselves away from the pressures of the day.

Ghostly Hands

Symbolises troubling thoughts.

Within a reading, the image of ghostly hands does not appear very often, but when it does it indicates that the sitter is being plagued with disturbing thoughts or unpleasant dreams. This is having a serious affect on the sitter, so they must get to the root of the problem that is causing these troubling thoughts or dreams and try to sort them out.

Pillar

Symbolises stability.

Within a reading, a pillar or pillars, represent strength, stability and balance. A single pillar can suggest that the sitter is the one who is supporting those around them, as in 'a pillar of strength'. When two pillars appear, usually at each side of the card, this could indicate that the sitter should consider their problems in a more diplomatic, or balanced way. Rather than left or right or black and white, the sitter should try to consider a more central view. In other words, the sitter should adopt a new perspective, a middle-of-the-road approach when tackling their problems.

Tassels

Symbolises achievement.

Within a reading, as tassels have always been associated with power, position and prestige, they are a good sign for the sitter. They foretell the achievement of desires or goals and as such, are a sign of success. They can also represent victory, or success over whatever hardships that the sitter is currently facing at the moment. If they stay resolute, they will overcome those hardships and come through it all successfully.

Window

Symbolises a new outlook.

Within a reading, a window represents a new perspective, or a new opportunity. However, it can also indicate that the sitter feels as if they are on the outside looking in. The time has come for the sitter to move inside and take an active part in whatever it is that they have been observing. Only by joining in will they be able to take advantage of all the new opportunities that will be within their grasp.

31 The Ten of Swords

Mountains

Symbolises challenges.

Within a reading, mountains usually appear in the background of the card. For the sitter, this suggests that they are facing seemingly insurmountable challenges, but that the sitter is trying to ignore them, pushing them to the back of their mind. If mountains appear in the majority of the spread, this indicates that the time has come for the sitter to face those challenges and to deal with them.

Path (Road)

Symbolises life choices.

Within a reading, a path or a road refers to the fact that the sitter is facing a new path in life. The sitter might be about to set out on that new path, or may already have taken their first few steps on it. Either way, this path represents a whole new and potentially exciting future for the sitter. If they are having any doubts about this new path, they shouldn't worry, as it will be the right choice for them.

Sea (Ocean)

Symbolises an unsettled time.

Within a reading, the appearance of the sea is designed to make us think about our life. The sitter should consider the vastness and the strength of the sea. It can be calm, but it can suddenly turn violent and unleash its power. For the sitter this can indicate that their life has recently been full of ups and downs, as situations ebb and flow through their recent daily routine. They probably feel as if they have recently been washed about from pillar to post. Calm will return, but they will have to be patient and ride out the storm.

32 The Page of Swords

Arch

Symbolises new beginnings.

Within a reading, the arch suggests that the sitter is about to take a new direction in life – whether they know it or not. A new opportunity is about to present itself to the sitter. This could be a new opening at work, a new career path for them to follow or possibly a new romantic involvement.

Clouds

Symbolises transition.

Within a reading, clouds have different meanings depending on what colour they are. In the suit of Swords, most of the clouds are dark and fast moving, representing that the sitter is probably going through a troublesome (or stormy) period in their life. However, dark clouds like these can also represent confusion, or clouded judgement.

Dark Skies (Storm Clouds)

Symbolises potential troubles.

Within a reading, the appearance of dark skies, or storm clouds, represents that the sitter is probably going through a rough patch in their life. On the other hand, dark skies, or stormy looking clouds, can also represent confusion about some issue in the sitter's life, or possibly that they are experiencing clouded judgement.

Feathers

Symbolises spiritual evolution.

Within a reading, a feather (or feathers) represents that the sitter is becoming aware of their spiritual side and that they are probably keen to advance that interest. Within the spiritual movement, feathers are universally recognised as a sign from Spirit, or a loved one that has passed.

Fur

Symbolises affluence, status and luxury.

Within a reading, animal fur depicts the sitter's desire for status, wealth and good fortune in life. However, in order to achieve those goals, the sitter will have to make some sacrifices.

Mountains

Symbolises challenges.

Within a reading, mountains usually appear in the background of the card. For the sitter, this suggests that they are facing seemingly insurmountable challenges, but that the sitter is trying to ignore them, pushing them to the back of their mind. If mountains appear in the majority of the spread, this indicates that the time has come for the sitter to face those challenges and to deal with them.

Ruff (Collar)

Symbolises stiffness of attitude.

Within a reading, the ruff was a stiffly starched decorative collar worn by the Elizabethans who believed that it displayed their mastery over their bodily sensations. For the present day sitter however, the meaning is a little less pompous. It can simply represent the fact that the sitter is being a little 'stiff-necked' about something. The time has come for the sitter to relax a bit, let go and enjoy life more.

Trees

Symbolises growth.

Within a reading, trees appear in many of the Tarot Cards, but significantly, they usually appear in the background. If trees appear in a lot of the cards within a spread, then this indicates that the sitter has plans for a new venture, path or phase in their life. However, at the moment, these plans are at the back of the sitter's mind. These plans are something that the sitter is considering putting into action in the near future, as they are still working on them, costing them out or carrying out research.

33 The Knight of Swords

Armour

Symbolises protection and strength.

Within a reading, the appearance of armour suggests that the sitter is feeling vulnerable in some way and that they feel the need to protect themselves from their perceived threat.

Clouds

Symbolises transition.

Within a reading, clouds have different meanings depending on what colour they are. In the suit of Swords, most of the clouds are dark and fast moving, representing that the sitter is probably going through a troublesome (or stormy) period in their life. However, dark clouds like these can also represent confusion, or clouded judgement.

Dark Skies (Storm Clouds)

Symbolises potential troubles.

Within a reading, the appearance of dark skies, or storm clouds, represents that the sitter is probably going through a rough patch in their life. On the other hand, dark skies, or stormy looking clouds, can also represent confusion about some issue in the sitter's life, or possibly that they are experiencing clouded judgement.

Eagle

Symbolises a connection to spiritual powers, Spirit Guides and Teachers.

Within a reading, the appearance of an eagle is a really good sign for any sitter who is trying to develop their psychic ability. It represents the fact that the sitter is doing well in their studies and that they will soon rise to the elevated heights that they are trying to achieve.

Fleur-de-lis

Symbolises adaptability.

Within a reading, some believe that the three shoots of the fleur-de-lis (a stylised lily) represent the Father, the Son and the Holy Spirit. Others prefer the representation of the unity of mind, body and spirit. Whichever representation you are drawn to, the three spreading shoots of the fleur-de-lis refer to the sitter's ability to adapt to changing circumstances.

Gauntlets (Gloves)

Symbolises a challenge.

Within a reading, the appearance of a gauntlet represents that the sitter is facing some kind of challenge in their life, as in 'throwing down the gauntlet'. This could be a challenge that they face, or a challenge that they have made.

Hawks

Symbolises freedom and growth.

Within a reading, the appearance of a hawk within a spread suggests that it is time for the sitter to free their minds from cluttered thoughts. It can also suggest that this is a time in the sitters life when they need to focus on what is ahead, as they might have to prepare for a future role of responsibility.

Horse

Symbolises strength and freedom.

Within a reading, a horse refers to the sitter's personal drive and a desire to free themselves from the current path that they are following. The sitter has the strength and stamina to easily achieve this goal, but they have to believe in themselves. Horses are also regarded as a deep spiritual sign, which might hint at the sitter's need for some spiritual guidance. Maybe the sitter needs to free themselves from old beliefs.

Mountains

Symbolises challenges.

Within a reading, mountains usually appear in the background of the card. For the sitter, this suggests that they are facing seemingly insurmountable challenges, but that the sitter is trying to ignore them, pushing them to the back of their mind. If mountains appear in the majority of the spread, this indicates that the time has come for the sitter to face those challenges and to deal with them.

Tassels

Symbolises achievement.

Within a reading, as tassels have always been associated with power, position and prestige, they are a good sign for the sitter. They foretell the achievement of desires or goals and as such, are a sign of success. They can also represent victory, or success over whatever hardships that the sitter is currently facing at the moment. If they stay resolute, they will overcome those hardships and come through it all successfully.

Tornado

Symbolises loss of control.

Within a reading, a tornado really isn't a good sign, as it represents upheaval in the sitter's life. This could be the sitter feeling overwhelmed by current events. Or possibly a feeling of losing control over their present situation. Whatever aspect of the sitter's life is going wrong for them, they are feeling that their life is spinning out of control and probably they are feeling a little helpless about it all. Now is the time for the sitter to take an in depth look at their situation and to take the necessary steps to regain control.

Trees

Symbolises growth.

Within a reading, trees appear in many of the Tarot Cards, but significantly, they usually appear in the background. If trees appear in a lot of the cards within a spread, then this indicates that the sitter has plans for a new venture, path or phase in their life. However, at the moment, these plans are at the back of the sitter's mind. These plans are something that the sitter is considering putting into action in the near future, as they are still working on them, costing them out or carrying out research.

Wings

Symbolises freedom.

Within a reading, wings represent a desire to be free. For the sitter, this could mean that they need the freedom to express themselves properly, or to act more freely in their life. It can also represent the need on the sitter's part to break free from whatever

constraints that are holding them back at the moment. If the wings are detached from the bird and attached to something else, this can infer that the sitter is being held back in some way. Someone or something has ‘clipped their wings’.
(If the wings are attached to an Angel, please go to the Angel Wings entry.)

34 The Queen of Swords

Angels

Symbolises divine messengers.

Within a reading, the appearance of an Angel in the spread represents that some kind of important information is coming the sitter's way. This could manifest itself in some sort of inspirational way, or even in a 'light bulb' moment. However the sitter receives this important information, they must not ignore it.

Arch

Symbolises new beginnings.

Within a reading, the arch suggests that the sitter is about to take a new direction in life – whether they know it or not. A new opportunity is about to present itself to the sitter. This could be a new opening at work, a new career path for them to follow or possibly a new romantic involvement.

Armour

Symbolises protection and strength.

Within a reading, the appearance of armour suggests that the sitter is feeling vulnerable in some way and that they feel the need to protect themselves from their perceived threat.

Butterfly

Symbolises transformation.

Within a reading, a butterfly suggests that it is time for the sitter to move away from their current phase in life to another, better phase. It can also represent that the sitter will have to change their way of thinking if they want to achieve their goals in life.

Clouds

Symbolises transition.

Within a reading, clouds have different meanings depending on what colour they are. In the suit of Swords, most of the clouds are dark and fast moving, representing that the sitter is probably going through a troublesome (or stormy) period in their life. However, dark clouds like these can also represent confusion, or clouded judgement.

Crown

Symbolises authority and power.

Within a reading, the appearance of a crown can signify many things. It could suggest that the sitter needs authority in their life. Possibly that the sitter desires recognition for their achievements. Or even that the sitter desires more control of their life, which might feel a little out of control to them at the moment.

Dark Skies (Storm Clouds)

Symbolises potential troubles.

Within a reading, the appearance of dark skies, or storm clouds, represents that the sitter is probably going through a rough patch in their life. On the other hand, dark skies, or stormy looking clouds, can also represent confusion about some issue in the sitter's life, or possibly that they are experiencing clouded judgement.

Fan

Symbolises stepping back and assessing the situation.

Within a reading, a fan represents that the sitter is more than likely feeling overwhelmed by their current situation. It is time for the sitter to 'cool it'. They need to take a break and assess their position before carrying on.

Throne

Symbolises stability.

Within a reading, as a throne is a seat of authority, this represents a position of responsibility for the sitter. Some aspect of the sitter's life is completely under their control. This could be a position at work, as in a managerial post. Possibly at home where the sitter has sole responsibility for raising a child or caring for someone for example. Whichever aspect of the sitter's life the throne refers to, it is running smoothly, but only because of the sitter's determination and steady hand.

Trees

Symbolises growth.

Within a reading, trees appear in many of the Tarot Cards, but significantly, they usually appear in the background. If trees appear in a lot of the cards within a spread, then this indicates that

the sitter has plans for a new venture, path or phase in their life. However, at the moment, these plans are at the back of the sitter's mind. These plans are something that the sitter is considering putting into action in the near future, as they are still working on them, costing them out or carrying out research.

Wings

Symbolises freedom.

Within a reading, wings represent a desire to be free. For the sitter, this could mean that they need the freedom to express themselves properly, or to act more freely in their life. It can also represent the need on the sitter's part to break free from whatever constraints that are holding them back at the moment. If the wings are detached from the bird and attached to something else, this can infer that the sitter is being held back in some way. Someone or something has 'clipped their wings'.

(If the wings are attached to an Angel, please go to the Angel Wings entry.)

35 The King of Swords

Axe Blades

Symbolises swift, but balanced justice.

Within a reading, axe blades suggest that the sitter is feeling inconvenienced or put out by recent events in their life. They are seeking a fast, but fair resolution to that problem.

Butterfly

Symbolises transformation.

Within a reading, a butterfly suggests that it is time for the sitter to move away from their current phase in life to another, better phase. It can also represent that the sitter will have to change their way of thinking if they want to achieve their goals in life.

Clouds

Symbolises transition.

Within a reading, clouds have different meanings depending on what colour they are. In the suit of Swords, most of the clouds are dark and fast moving, representing that the sitter is probably going through a troublesome (or stormy) period in their life. However, dark clouds like these can also represent confusion, or clouded judgement.

Crown

Symbolises authority and power.

Within a reading, the appearance of a crown can signify many things. It could suggest that the sitter needs authority in their life. Possibly that the sitter desires recognition for their achievements. Or even that the sitter desires more control of their life, which might feel a little out of control to them at the moment.

Dark Skies (Storm Clouds)

Symbolises potential troubles.

Within a reading, the appearance of dark skies, or storm clouds, represents that the sitter is probably going through a rough patch in their life. On the other hand, dark skies, or stormy looking clouds, can also represent confusion about some issue in the sitter's life, or possibly that they are experiencing clouded judgement.

Eagle

Symbolises a connection to spiritual powers, Spirit Guides and Teachers.

Within a reading, the appearance of an eagle is a really good sign for any sitter who is trying to develop their psychic ability. It represents the fact that the sitter is doing well in their studies and that they will soon rise to the elevated heights that they are trying to achieve.

Fur

Symbolises affluence, status and luxury.

Within a reading, animal fur depicts the sitter's desire for status, wealth and good fortune in life. However, in order to achieve those goals, the sitter will have to make some sacrifices.

Infinity Symbol

Symbolises endless possibilities.

Within a reading, the Infinity Symbol (The Lemniscate) represents the never-ending possibilities in our lives. For the sitter, it implies that they possess the necessary endless energy to face whatever life throws at them. It can also represent everlasting love.

Pillar

Symbolises stability.

Within a reading, a pillar or pillars, represent strength, stability and balance. A single pillar can suggest that the sitter is the one who is supporting those around them, as in 'a pillar of strength'. When two pillars appear, usually at each side of the card, this could indicate that the sitter should consider their problems in a more diplomatic, or balanced way. Rather than left or right or black and white, the sitter should try to consider a more central view. In other words, the sitter should adopt a new perspective, a middle-of-the-road approach when tackling their problems.

Throne

Symbolises stability.

Within a reading, as a throne is a seat of authority, this represents a position of responsibility for the sitter. Some aspect of the sitter's life is completely under their control. This could be a position at work, as in a managerial post. Possibly at home where the sitter has sole responsibility for raising a child or caring for someone for example. Whichever aspect of the sitter's life the throne refers to, it is running smoothly, but only because of the sitter's determination and steady hand.

Trees

Symbolises growth.

Within a reading, trees appear in many of the Tarot Cards, but significantly, they usually appear in the background. If trees appear in a lot of the cards within a spread, then this indicates that the sitter has plans for a new venture, path or phase in their life. However, at the moment, these plans are at the back of the sitter's mind. These plans are something that the sitter is considering putting into action in the near future, as they are still working on them, costing them out or carrying out research.

Wings

Symbolises freedom.

Within a reading, wings represent a desire to be free. For the sitter, this could mean that they need the freedom to express themselves properly, or to act more freely in their life. It can also represent the need on the sitter's part to break free from whatever constraints that are holding them back at the moment. If the wings are detached from the bird and attached to something else, this can infer that the sitter is being held back in some way. Someone or something has 'clipped their wings'.

(If the wings are attached to an Angel, please go to the Angel Wings entry.)

36 The Ace of Cups

Bird

Any species of bird symbolises rising above the normal.

Within a reading, a bird represents the sitter's need to lighten their thoughts. To rise above the problems of the material world and to look at the bigger picture. A bird can also symbolise the sitter's need to look at and to raise their individual spirituality.

Clouds

Symbolises transition.

Within a reading, clouds have different meanings depending on what colour they are. In the suit of Swords, most of the clouds are dark and fast moving, representing that the sitter is probably going through a troublesome (or stormy) period in their life. However, dark clouds like these can also represent confusion, or clouded judgement.

Coral

Symbolises abundance and prosperity.

Within a reading, the appearance of coral in the spread indicates that the sitter is enjoying the fruits of their labours. However, just like the coral itself, their current situation could be more fragile than they might realise. It is important that the sitter takes steps to protect themselves.

Dove

Symbolises peace, purity and love.

Within a reading, a dove can represent many things. It is a symbol of peace and love, but it is also regarded by many as a true spiritual sign. If the sitter has been experiencing a troubling time recently, the dove can be regarded as a sign that their troubles will soon be over and that peace and tranquillity will soon be restored.

Fish

Symbolises intuition and creativity.

Within a reading, fish have many meanings. Fish can represent knowledge, inspiration or the mental balancing of the sitter's thoughts. The sitter might be a very creative person, or might possess a high level of intuition or spiritual ability. On the other hand, it could represent the fact that the sitter is involved with, or is dealing with a 'slippery' person or situation.

Goblet/Chalice

Symbolises family and tradition.

Within a reading, the appearance of a goblet or chalice indicates that family is extremely important to the sitter. It implies that the sitter probably possesses a pretty traditional view of what family life means to them. In particular, children and grandchildren mean everything to them and are their very reason for being.

Hand

Symbolises transmission or give and take.

Within a reading, a hand or a pair of hands on their own implies that the sitter should understand that the problem that they are dealing with at this moment in their life, can only be solved with some kind of compromise. Hands give and receive, or give and take, so should the sitter.

Sea (Ocean)

Symbolises an unsettled time.

Within a reading, the appearance of the sea is designed to make us think about our life. The sitter should consider the vastness and the strength of the sea. It can be calm, but it can suddenly turn violent and unleash its power. For the sitter this can indicate that their life has recently been full of ups and downs, as situations ebb and flow through their recent daily routine. They probably feel as if they have recently been washed about from pillar to post. Calm will return, but they will have to be patient and ride out the storm.

Water

Symbolises cleansing.

Within a reading, water usually represents the need for the sitter to 'cleanse' themselves. Not in the physical sense of needing a wash, but in an emotional or spiritual sense. In other words, the sitter needs to 'wash away' whatever it is that is troubling them. This would normally be an old memory, experience or episode in their life that is holding the sitter back. Once they have removed the issues that are bothering them, they will feel reborn and ready to move on with their life.

37 The Two of Cups

Caduceus

Symbolises balance, harmony, renewal and transformation.

Within a reading, a caduceus represents that the sitter is going through, or is about to go through a transitional stage in their life. Whatever this change may be, it will be beneficial to the sitter, bringing peace, balance and harmony into their life. Bodes well for new relationships.

Crab

Symbolises perseverance and tenacity.

Within a reading, a crab can represent that the sitter might be clinging on to a hopeless or useless endeavour. They need to take a 'sideways' step and examine the situation in order to work out if the endeavour is worth the effort.

Female Symbol

Symbolises femininity.

Within a reading, the female sign obviously relates to femininity. However, if the sitter is a male, he should try and get in touch with his feminine side.

Goblet/Chalice

Symbolises family and tradition.

Within a reading, the appearance of a goblet or chalice indicates that family is extremely important to the sitter. It implies that the sitter probably possesses a pretty traditional view of what family life means to them. In particular, children and grandchildren mean everything to them and are their very reason for being.

Hills

Symbolises obstacles.

Within a reading, the appearance of hills in the spread suggests that the sitter is facing obstacles in their life that they need to overcome. However daunting or impossible these hurdles might appear to be for the sitter, they need to remove these obstacles in their life in order to move on.

Lion

Symbolises courage and strength.

Within a reading, a lion can indicate that the sitter has the necessary personal courage and emotional strength required to overcome the difficulties that they are facing right now. Just as the lion is fearless, it is time for the sitter to conquer his or her own fears. Fear can hold us back, so conquering your fears will is the key to the sitter achieving the success that they desire.

Pearls

Symbolises wisdom.

Within a reading, pearls are said to represent wisdom that has been acquired through experience. As far as the sitter is concerned, pearls infer that he or she has learned a life lesson recently, having gone through an experience that was probably an unpleasant one. As the saying goes, 'wise after the event'. However, this newly gained wisdom will prepare them for similar future events and allow them to handle it better.

Tassels

Symbolises achievement.

Within a reading, as tassels have always been associated with power, position and prestige, they are a good sign for the sitter. They foretell the achievement of desires or goals and as such, are a sign of success. They can also represent victory, or success over whatever hardships that the sitter is currently facing at the moment. If they stay resolute, they will overcome those hardships and come through it all successfully.

Water

Symbolises cleansing.

Within a reading, water usually represents the need for the sitter to 'cleanse' themselves. Not in the physical sense of needing a wash, but in an emotional or spiritual sense. In other words, the sitter needs to 'wash away' whatever it is that is troubling them. This would normally be an old memory, experience or episode in their life that is holding the sitter back. Once they have removed the issues that are bothering them, they will feel reborn and ready to move on with their life.

Wings

Symbolises freedom.

Within a reading, wings represent a desire to be free. For the sitter, this could mean that they need the freedom to express themselves properly, or to act more freely in their life. It can also represent the need on the sitter's part to break free from whatever constraints that are holding them back at the moment. If the wings are detached from the bird and attached to something else, this can infer that the sitter is being held back in some way. Someone or something has 'clipped their wings'.

(If the wings are attached to an Angel, please go to the Angel Wings entry.)

38 The Three of Cups

Apple

Symbolises love, joy or knowledge.

Within a reading, the appearance of an apple suggests that the sitter is about to 'take a bite' out of that apple. This could represent the sitter is about to begin a new relationship, or that they are about to begin a new course of study.

Flowers

Symbolises new life and regeneration.

Within a reading, different individual flowers have different meanings. However, flowers in general represent that the sitter is opening (or has already opened) themselves up to new ideas, beliefs or experiences, all of which they will benefit from.

Goblet/Chalice

Symbolises family and tradition.

Within a reading, the appearance of a goblet or chalice indicates that family is extremely important to the sitter. It implies that the sitter probably possesses a pretty traditional view of what family life means to them. In particular, children and grandchildren mean everything to them and are their very reason for being.

Grapes (Grapevines)

Symbolises bountifulness.

Within a reading, grapes or grapevines imply that the sitter is a very hospitable and generous person, who enjoys sharing the fruits of their bounty (work or good fortune) with others. Can also signify abundance and fertility within the sitter's life.

Sea (Ocean)

Symbolises an unsettled time.

Within a reading, the appearance of the sea is designed to make us think about our life. The sitter should consider the vastness and the strength of the sea. It can be calm, but it can suddenly turn violent and unleash its power. For the sitter this can indicate that their life has recently been full of ups and downs, as situations ebb and flow through their recent daily routine. They probably feel as if they have recently been washed about from pillar to post. Calm will return, but they will have to be patient and ride out the storm.

39 The Four of Cups

Acorns

Symbolises life, fertility and regeneration.

Within a reading, an acorn can indicate that the sitter is undergoing a new phase in their life. They are possibly about to enter a new phase of personal growth. This could be within their personal or professional life. The acorn can represent the germination of a new idea that can only grow stronger.

Clouds

Symbolises transition.

Within a reading, clouds have different meanings depending on what colour they are. In the suit of Swords, most of the clouds are dark and fast moving, representing that the sitter is probably going through a troublesome (or stormy) period in their life. However, dark clouds like these can also represent confusion, or clouded judgement.

Goblet/Chalice

Symbolises family and tradition.

Within a reading, the appearance of a goblet or chalice indicates that family is extremely important to the sitter. It implies that the sitter probably possesses a pretty traditional view of what family life means to them. In particular, children and grandchildren mean everything to them and are their very reason for being.

Rock

Symbolises dependability.

Within a reading, the appearance of a rock (or rocks) suggests that the sitter is one of life's more dependable souls. Their passion and determination is apparent in everything that they do. It shows that they have the personal strength to overcome the situations that life throws at them. The old sayings 'as solid as a rock' and 'he/she is my rock' definitely apply to this sitter.

Trees

Symbolises growth.

Within a reading, trees appear in many of the Tarot Cards, but significantly, they usually appear in the background. If trees appear in a lot of the cards within a spread, then this indicates that

the sitter has plans for a new venture, path or phase in their life. However, at the moment, these plans are at the back of the sitter’s mind. These plans are something that the sitter is considering putting into action in the near future, as they are still working on them, costing them out or carrying out research.

40 The Five of Cups

Brick Wall

Symbolises a self-imposed barrier, or mental block.

Within a reading, a brick wall represents that the sitter is separating themselves from a problem, trying to shut that problem out of their mind. It is reluctance on the sitter's part to acknowledge what is happening around them. It can also represent the sitter holding themselves back or doubting themselves.

Bridge

Symbolises dwelling on the past.

Within a reading, the appearance of a bridge represents the sitter's mind being stuck in past events. The bridge is a reminder to the sitter that it is time to move on to a new phase in their life.

Broken Glass

Symbolises that something is beyond repair.

Within a reading, the appearance of broken or shattered glass represents a final (and probably permanent) break in the sitter's life. This could be anything from the end of a relationship to the end of their current occupation.

Castle

Symbolises goals and achievements.

Within a reading, a castle represents the sitter's long and difficult journey to achieve their goal in life. This might be a long university degree course, or a long battle against illness. Whatever the sitter's goal is, they are well on their way to achieving it. On a simpler note, a castle can represent security or sanctuary.

Cliff Edge

Signifies possible new opportunities.

Within a reading, a cliff edge can represent two things. The sitter is about to embark on a new path, which has been created by the arrival of a new opportunity in their life. On one hand, this is an exciting time for the sitter. On the other hand, they should take precautions, as there are potential pitfalls ahead.

Goblet/Chalice

Symbolises family and tradition.

Within a reading, the appearance of a goblet or chalice indicates that family is extremely important to the sitter. It implies that the sitter probably possesses a pretty traditional view of what family life means to them. In particular, children and grandchildren mean everything to them and are their very reason for being.

River

Symbolises obstacles.

Within a reading, the appearance of a river can be interpreted in two different ways. For the sitter, a river can represent an obstacle that they have to get across, as it is blocking their path or progress. On the other hand, it could be advising the sitter to stop struggling with whatever problem that they are facing or dealing with. It is time for them to 'go with the flow' and let the problem resolve itself.

Rock

Symbolises dependability.

Within a reading, the appearance of a rock (or rocks) suggests that the sitter is one of life's more dependable souls. Their passion and determination is apparent in everything that they do. It shows that they have the personal strength to overcome the situations that life throws at them. The old sayings 'as solid as a rock' and 'he/she is my rock' definitely apply to this sitter.

Sea (Ocean)

Symbolises an unsettled time.

Within a reading, the appearance of the sea is designed to make us think about our life. The sitter should consider the vastness and the strength of the sea. It can be calm, but it can suddenly turn violent and unleash its power. For the sitter this can indicate that their life has recently been full of ups and downs, as situations ebb and flow through their recent daily routine. They probably feel as if they have recently been washed about from pillar to post. Calm will return, but they will have to be patient and ride out the storm.

Teardrops

Symbolises sorrows.

Within a reading, the appearance of teardrops within a spread indicates that the sitter is going through a painful process of some description at the moment. This could be anything from the recent loss of a loved one, up to being plagued with painful memories of an incident from their past. It might take time, but the sitter will get over these sorrows. They can speed up the process if they can learn how to alter the way that they think.

Wall

Symbolises barriers.

Within a reading, a wall represents building a barrier in life. For the sitter, this refers to them needing to separate one area of their life from another. The surrounding cards should give an indication as to what areas need separating. It can also suggest that the sitter is holding back in some way, hiding behind a wall of their own making. However, a wall can also suggest quite simply that the sitter is in need of some privacy.

41 The Six of Cups

Brick Wall

Symbolises a self-imposed barrier, or mental block.

Within a reading, a brick wall represents that the sitter is separating themselves from a problem, trying to shut that problem out of their mind. It is reluctance on the sitter's part to acknowledge what is happening around them. It can also represent the sitter holding themselves back or doubting themselves.

Child/Children

Symbolises innocence and memories.

Within a reading, a child or children appearing in the spread signifies that the sitter might be living in the past too much. Childhood memories can be happy or sad, but should never be dwelled upon. However, children in the tarot can also represent promise for the future, or the beginning of a new venture, as well as a child-like enthusiasm for life.

Flowers

Symbolises new life and regeneration.

Within a reading, different individual flowers have different meanings. However, flowers in general represent that the sitter is opening (or has already opened) themselves up to new ideas, beliefs or experiences, all of which they will benefit from.

Goblet/Chalice

Symbolises family and tradition.

Within a reading, the appearance of a goblet or chalice indicates that family is extremely important to the sitter. It implies that the sitter probably possesses a pretty traditional view of what family life means to them. In particular, children and grandchildren mean everything to them and are their very reason for being.

House (Cottage)

Symbolises safety and security.

Within a reading, houses or cottages usually appear in the background of the card. This implies that for the sitter (as for all of us) their home is always in the back of their mind. Our homes are our places of sanctuary in our increasingly fast-paced and busy lives. For the sitter, home is where the heart is and they probably wish that they could spend more time there, implying that maybe they are working too hard and too many long hours.

Kite

Symbolises aspirations.

Within a reading, a kite can represent the sitter's hopes, dreams and aspirations. However, it ca also represent the sitter's desire to escape their responsibilities.

Sunset

Symbolises an ending.

Within a reading, the image of a sunset infers that some aspect of the sitter's life is winding down or coming to an end. This could be a period of intense work, a difficult phase, a troubling time or maybe just the end of a project that has taken longer to complete than anticipated. Whatever it is that is coming to an end, it is now time for the sitter to relax, as the worst is now over.

Wall

Symbolises barriers.

Within a reading, a wall represents building a barrier in life. For the sitter, this refers to them needing to separate one area of their life from another. The surrounding cards should give an indication as to what areas need separating. It can also suggest that the sitter is holding back in some way, hiding behind a wall of their own making. However, a wall can also suggest quite simply that the sitter is in need of some privacy.

42 The Seven of Cups

Castle

Symbolises goals and achievements.

Within a reading, a castle represents the sitter's long and difficult journey to achieve their goal in life. This might be a long university degree course, or a long battle against illness. Whatever the sitter's goal is, they are well on their way to achieving it. On a simpler note, a castle can represent security or sanctuary.

Clouds

Symbolises transition.

Within a reading, clouds have different meanings depending on what colour they are. In the suit of Swords, most of the clouds are dark and fast moving, representing that the sitter is probably going through a troublesome (or stormy) period in their life. However, dark clouds like these can also represent confusion, or clouded judgement.

Crown

Symbolises authority and power.

Within a reading, the appearance of a crown can signify many things. It could suggest that the sitter needs authority in their life. Possibly that the sitter desires recognition for their achievements. Or even that the sitter desires more control of their life, which might feel a little out of control to them at the moment.

Dragon

Symbolises wisdom, strength and courage.

Within a reading, the appearance of a dragon in the spread represents that the sitter needs to rise over their present circumstances in order to see things more clearly. Whatever their currant problem is, they need moral strength and personal courage to overcome it.

Fairy

Symbolises paranormal powers and imagination.

Within a reading, the appearance of a fairy in the spread indicates that the sitter probably possesses psychic abilities, whether they are aware of it or not. The images that flash through their minds are being wrongly dismissed as simple imagination.

Goblet/Chalice

Symbolises family and tradition.

Within a reading, the appearance of a goblet or chalice indicates that family is extremely important to the sitter. It implies that the sitter probably possesses a pretty traditional view of what family life means to them. In particular, children and grandchildren mean everything to them and are their very reason for being.

Jewellery

Symbolises financial security.

Within a reading, the appearance of jewellery can suggest that the sitter has a desire, or a need for financial security. It can also represent the sitter's aspirations for wealth. The sitter probably has a plan forming in their mind regarding how they can improve their financial status.

Laurel Wreath

Symbolises achievement.

Within a reading, the appearance of a laurel wreath indicates that the sitter has recently achieved something in their life that they are very proud of. This could be anything from passing an exam, getting the job that they have always wanted or overcoming some personal problem that has been holding them back.

Octopus

Symbolises flexibility.

Within a reading, an octopus has nearly as many meanings as the octopus has tentacles. It can represent flexibility, unpredictability or even creativity. However, as far as the sitter is concerned, it is probably a warning to cut back on their workload and responsibilities, as they have their fingers in too many pies and the strain is starting to tell on them.

Rainbow

Symbolises success and hope.

Within a reading, the shape of a rainbow can appear to resemble a bridge. This is significant for the sitter, as it implies that he or she has some bridges to build or repair in their life. This could be bridges in their professional or private lives. Now is the time to start, as the basic symbolism of a rainbow is success and joy.

Snake

Symbolises transformation.

Within a reading, a snake can symbolise renewal and rebirth, because it sheds its skin and re-emerges ready for its next phase in life. For the sitter, this can indicate that they should probably ask themselves if they need to 'shed' some part of themselves. Shedding some negative aspect of their life will allow them to grow and move on. A snake can also represent the fact that the sitter should be on the alert for so-called friends who really do not have their best interests at heart, a 'snake in the grass' so to speak.

Star (Stars)

Symbolises guidance.

Within a reading, the appearance of stars in the spread indicates that the sitter is experiencing some turmoil in their life at the moment. Their life seems to be a little topsy-turvy right now, causing them a lot of confusion. The star symbol deals with shedding some light into their life. They must focus on one problem at a time and deal with it, moving onto the next problem and dealing with that and so on. There is light at the end of the tunnel, but the illumination of that light comes from within.

Veil

Symbolises mysticism.

Within a reading, a veil can represent two sides of the same coin. On the one hand, a veil can indicate that the sitter is hiding behind a façade, not allowing the world to see the real person inside. On the other hand, a veil can represent that the sitter possesses hidden knowledge, usually of a spiritual or psychic nature. Either way, the sitter sits behind a veil of mysticism and is usually an old soul with life experiences beyond their years.

43 The Eight of Cups

Castle

Symbolises goals and achievements.

Within a reading, a castle represents the sitter's long and difficult journey to achieve their goal in life. This might be a long university degree course, or a long battle against illness. Whatever the sitter's goal is, they are well on their way to achieving it. On a simpler note, a castle can represent security or sanctuary.

Goblet/Chalice

Symbolises family and tradition.

Within a reading, the appearance of a goblet or chalice indicates that family is extremely important to the sitter. It implies that the sitter probably possesses a pretty traditional view of what family life means to them. In particular, children and grandchildren mean everything to them and are their very reason for being.

Moon

Symbolises cycles.

Within a reading, the appearance of the moon in a spread indicates that the sitter is moving from one phase of their life to another. Whatever transition is taking place in the sitter's life, it is for the sitter's overall good and/or wellbeing. The moon can also indicate that the sitter is quite a spiritual person, who might very well be starting to realise that they have psychic abilities themselves.

Mountains

Symbolises challenges.

Within a reading, mountains usually appear in the background of the card. For the sitter, this suggests that they are facing seemingly insurmountable challenges, but that the sitter is trying to ignore them, pushing them to the back of their mind. If mountains appear in the majority of the spread, this indicates that the time has come for the sitter to face those challenges and to deal with them.

Octopus

Symbolises flexibility.

Within a reading, an octopus has nearly as many meanings as the octopus has tentacles. It can represent flexibility, unpredictability or even creativity. However, as far as the sitter is concerned, it is probably a warning to cut back on their workload and responsibilities, as they have their fingers in too many pies and the strain is starting to tell on them.

River

Symbolises obstacles.

Within a reading, the appearance of a river can be interpreted in two different ways. For the sitter, a river can represent an obstacle that they have to get across, as it is blocking their path or progress. On the other hand, it could be advising the sitter to stop struggling with whatever problem that they are facing or dealing with. It is time for them to 'go with the flow' and let the problem resolve itself.

Waterfall

Symbolises letting go.

Within a reading, a waterfall indicates that the time has come for the sitter to rid themselves (to let go) of something that is holding them back. This could be events in their past, some negative thoughts or some belief that used to be very important to them. Just as the waterfall sweeps away all of the detritus that it encounters along its way, the sitter should do the same. Letting go of these emotions, worries or memories will set them free to enjoy a new and uncluttered phase in their life.

44 The Nine of Cups

Bench

Symbolises the need to study the details.

Within a reading, a bench represents the need for the sitter to take their time and to examine the details of the situation that they currently find themselves in. Symbolically 'laying out the plans' and studying them.

Chains

Symbolises restraint or restriction.

Within a reading, chains represent that the sitter is feeling held back, or being prevented from carrying out some action or other. If the chains are presented as some form of jewellery, then the sitter's problem is of a more delicate nature.

Coconuts

Symbolises self-protection and self-projection.

Within a reading, a coconut represents that the sitter is displaying a tough 'outer shell', or public face to the world in an effort to protect themselves. They are however pretending that they are tougher than they really are. It will do the sitter no harm to allow their softer, inner self to made known to those around them.

Fruit

Symbolises good health and love.

Within a reading, any fruit can represent that the sitter has started out on a new path in life. All fruits have seeds and those seeds, when plated, will grow. (The 'seed' of a new idea for example.) so any fruit represents growth and new beginnings for the sitter. Also, as a symbol of fertility, fruit can represent pregnancy.

Goblet/Chalice

Symbolises family and tradition.

Within a reading, the appearance of a goblet or chalice indicates that family is extremely important to the sitter. It implies that the sitter probably possesses a pretty traditional view of what family life means to them. In particular, children and grandchildren mean everything to them and are their very reason for being.

Gold Chain of Office

Symbolises position and authority.

Within a reading, a gold chain of office (as opposed to a gold necklace) implies that the sitter is chasing after, or has recently achieved a long sought after role in life. This could be a promotion at their present place of employment, or possibly a new job that they have recently started.

Nuts

Symbolises toughness.

Within a reading, the appearance of any kind of nut usually represents toughness due to their hard outer shell. For the sitter however, this can symbolise that the time has come for them to toughen up in some way. It might be difficult for them to change their basic nature in this way, but it must be done if they wish to succeed with their present plans.

45 The Ten of Cups

Cat

Symbolises spiritual ability.

Within a reading, the appearance of a cat in the spread denotes the sitter's quest for spiritual enlightenment. Not necessarily in a religious sense (although it could be), but possibly just seeking a path in life that can liberate them and make them feel free. In this case, a cat would indicate that the sitter is burdened with too many responsibilities.

Chains

Symbolises restraint or restriction.

Within a reading, chains represent that the sitter is feeling held back, or being prevented from carrying out some action or other. If the chains are presented as some form of jewellery, then the sitter's problem is of a more delicate nature.

Child/Children

Symbolises innocence and memories.

Within a reading, a child or children appearing in the spread signifies that the sitter might be living in the past too much. Childhood memories can be happy or sad, but should never be dwelled upon. However, children in the tarot can also represent promise for the future, or the beginning of a new venture, as well as a child-like enthusiasm for life.

Dog/Dogs

Symbolises loyalty or devotion.

Within a reading, whenever a dog (or dogs) appear in the spread it represents that the sitter might be experiencing loyalty issues. However, a dog can also represent that the sitter is on the right track in life, as dogs are symbolic of stability and steadfastness.

Fire (Flames)

Symbolises transformation.

Within a reading, fire or flames represents that the sitter is going through some kind of transition in their life. They can also represent that the sitter might need to make some kind of change, alteration or modification to their lifestyle.

Flowers

Symbolises new life and regeneration.

Within a reading, different individual flowers have different meanings. However, flowers in general represent that the sitter is opening (or has already opened) themselves up to new ideas, beliefs or experiences, all of which they will benefit from.

Goblet/Chalice

Symbolises family and tradition.

Within a reading, the appearance of a goblet or chalice indicates that family is extremely important to the sitter. It implies that the sitter probably possesses a pretty traditional view of what family life means to them. In particular, children and grandchildren mean everything to them and are their very reason for being.

House (Cottage)

Symbolises safety and security.

Within a reading, houses or cottages usually appear in the background of the card. This implies that for the sitter (as for all of us) their home is always in the back of their mind. Our homes are our places of sanctuary in our increasingly fast-paced and busy lives. For the sitter, home is where the heart is and they probably wish that they could spend more time there, implying that maybe they are working too hard and too many long hours.

Rainbow

Symbolises success and hope.

Within a reading, the shape of a rainbow can appear to resemble a bridge. This is significant for the sitter, as it implies that he or she has some bridges to build or repair in their life. This could be bridges in their professional or private lives. Now is the time to start, as the basic symbolism of a rainbow is success and joy.

River

Symbolises obstacles.

Within a reading, the appearance of a river can be interpreted in two different ways. For the sitter, a river can represent an obstacle that they have to get across, as it is blocking their path or progress. On the other hand, it could be advising the sitter to stop struggling with whatever problem that they are facing or dealing with. It is time for them to 'go with the flow' and let the problem resolve itself.

Trees

Symbolises growth.

Within a reading, trees appear in many of the Tarot Cards, but significantly, they usually appear in the background. If trees appear in a lot of the cards within a spread, then this indicates that the sitter has plans for a new venture, path or phase in their life. However, at the moment, these plans are at the back of the sitter's mind. These plans are something that the sitter is considering putting into action in the near future, as they are still working on them, costing them out or carrying out research.

46 The Page of Cups

Feathers

Symbolises spiritual evolution.

Within a reading, a feather (or feathers) represents that the sitter is becoming aware of their spiritual side and that they are probably keen to advance that interest. Within the spiritual movement, feathers are universally recognised as a sign from Spirit, or a loved one that has passed.

Fish

Symbolises intuition and creativity.

Within a reading, fish have many meanings. Fish can represent knowledge, inspiration or the mental balancing of the sitter's thoughts. The sitter might be a very creative person, or might possess a high level of intuition or spiritual ability. On the other hand, it could represent the fact that the sitter is involved with, or is dealing with a 'slippery' person or situation.

Goblet/Chalice

Symbolises family and tradition.

Within a reading, the appearance of a goblet or chalice indicates that family is extremely important to the sitter. It implies that the sitter probably possesses a pretty traditional view of what family life means to them. In particular, children and grandchildren mean everything to them and are their very reason for being.

Sea (Ocean)

Symbolises an unsettled time.

Within a reading, the appearance of the sea is designed to make us think about our life. The sitter should consider the vastness and the strength of the sea. It can be calm, but it can suddenly turn violent and unleash its power. For the sitter this can indicate that their life has recently been full of ups and downs, as situations ebb and flow through their recent daily routine. They probably feel as if they have recently been washed about from pillar to post. Calm will return, but they will have to be patient and ride out the storm.

Shells

Symbolises protection.

Within a reading, the appearance of any kind of shell can infer that the sitter is feeling a little vulnerable at the moment. This could be an emotional, financial or an employment situation that is causing the sitter worry. Whatever is causing trouble for the sitter, he or she needs to prepare for this situation and put a defensive barrier in place, a 'protective shell' to fend off whatever is happening to them at the moment, or for whatever is coming their way.

Triangle

Symbolises strength.

Within a reading, the triangle is the strongest basic geometric shape known to man, which is why it is used to support a roof in a domestic building for example. It is this very strength of the triangle which is significant in a reading. It infers that the sitter has a strong character, as in moral strength rather than physical strength. Whatever life throws at this particular sitter, they can handle it.

47 The Knight of Cups

Armour

Symbolises protection and strength.

Within a reading, the appearance of armour suggests that the sitter is feeling vulnerable in some way and that they feel the need to protect themselves from their perceived threat.

Coral

Symbolises abundance and prosperity.

Within a reading, the appearance of coral in the spread indicates that the sitter is enjoying the fruits of their labours. However, just like the coral itself, their current situation could be more fragile than they might realise. It is important that the sitter takes steps to protect themselves.

Fish

Symbolises intuition and creativity.

Within a reading, fish have many meanings. Fish can represent knowledge, inspiration or the mental balancing of the sitter's thoughts. The sitter might be a very creative person, or might possess a high level of intuition or spiritual ability. On the other hand, it could represent the fact that the sitter is involved with, or is dealing with a 'slippery' person or situation.

Goblet/Chalice

Symbolises family and tradition.

Within a reading, the appearance of a goblet or chalice indicates that family is extremely important to the sitter. It implies that the sitter probably possesses a pretty traditional view of what family life means to them. In particular, children and grandchildren mean everything to them and are their very reason for being.

Helmet

Symbolises protection.

Within a reading, a helmet can suggest that the sitter is feeling vulnerable in some way and is looking for a way to protect themselves from the cause. Usually a helmet has a plume or crest on top of it for identification. This could suggest that the sitter is searching for acceptance in some way.

Horse

Symbolises strength and freedom.

Within a reading, a horse refers to the sitter's personal drive and a desire to free themselves from the current path that they are following. The sitter has the strength and stamina to easily achieve this goal, but they have to believe in themselves. Horses are also regarded as a deep spiritual sign, which might hint at the sitter's need for some spiritual guidance. Maybe the sitter needs to free themselves from old beliefs.

Manta Rays

Symbolises grace and flow.

Within a reading, the appearance of a manta ray is quite rare, but it represents grace, flow and wisdom. As manta rays are sensitive to the flows of the ocean's energy, it is a reminder to the sitter that they should start to tune into the flow of their own spiritual energy.

Mountains

Symbolises challenges.

Within a reading, mountains usually appear in the background of the card. For the sitter, this suggests that they are facing seemingly insurmountable challenges, but that the sitter is trying to ignore them, pushing them to the back of their mind. If mountains appear in the majority of the spread, this indicates that the time has come for the sitter to face those challenges and to deal with them.

River

Symbolises obstacles.

Within a reading, the appearance of a river can be interpreted in two different ways. For the sitter, a river can represent an obstacle that they have to get across, as it is blocking their path or progress. On the other hand, it could be advising the sitter to stop struggling with whatever problem that they are facing or dealing with. It is time for them to 'go with the flow' and let the problem resolve itself.

Sea (Ocean)

Symbolises an unsettled time.

Within a reading, the appearance of the sea is designed to make us think about our life. The sitter should consider the vastness and the strength of the sea. It can be calm, but it can suddenly turn violent and unleash its power. For the sitter this can indicate that their life has recently been full of ups and downs, as situations ebb and flow through their recent daily routine. They probably feel as if they have recently been washed about from pillar to post. Calm will return, but they will have to be patient and ride out the storm.

Tassels

Symbolises achievement.

Within a reading, as tassels have always been associated with power, position and prestige, they are a good sign for the sitter. They foretell the achievement of desires or goals and as such, are a sign of success. They can also represent victory, or success over whatever hardships that the sitter is currently facing at the moment. If they stay resolute, they will overcome those hardships and come through it all successfully.

Trees

Symbolises growth.

Within a reading, trees appear in many of the Tarot Cards, but significantly, they usually appear in the background. If trees appear in a lot of the cards within a spread, then this indicates that the sitter has plans for a new venture, path or phase in their life. However, at the moment, these plans are at the back of the sitter's mind. These plans are something that the sitter is considering putting into action in the near future, as they are still working on them, costing them out or carrying out research.

Wings

Symbolises freedom.

Within a reading, wings represent a desire to be free. For the sitter, this could mean that they need the freedom to express themselves properly, or to act more freely in their life. It can also represent the need on the sitter's part to break free from whatever

constraints that are holding them back at the moment. If the wings are detached from the bird and attached to something else, this can infer that the sitter is being held back in some way. Someone or something has 'clipped their wings'.
(If the wings are attached to an Angel, please go to the Angel Wings entry.)

48 The Queen of Cups

Arm Band

Symbolises belonging.

Within a reading, an armband represents the need of the sitter to belong to something. This might be a group or organisation that the sitter feels attracted to.
(An armband can be a piece of material, a piece of jewellery or even a tattoo.)

Cherubs

Symbolises spiritual innocence.

Within a reading, a cherub can represent the sitter's innocence or naivety in the adult world. It could also represent that the sitter is one of life's gentler souls.

Crown

Symbolises authority and power.

Within a reading, the appearance of a crown can signify many things. It could suggest that the sitter needs authority in their life. Possibly that the sitter desires recognition for their achievements. Or even that the sitter desires more control of their life, which might feel a little out of control to them at the moment.

Fish

Symbolises intuition and creativity.

Within a reading, fish have many meanings. Fish can represent knowledge, inspiration or the mental balancing of the sitter's thoughts. The sitter might be a very creative person, or might possess a high level of intuition or spiritual ability. On the other hand, it could represent the fact that the sitter is involved with, or is dealing with a 'slippery' person or situation.

Goblet/Chalice

Symbolises family and tradition.

Within a reading, the appearance of a goblet or chalice indicates that family is extremely important to the sitter. It implies that the sitter probably possesses a pretty traditional view of what family life means to them. In particular, children and grandchildren mean everything to them and are their very reason for being.

Pearls

Symbolises wisdom.

Within a reading, pearls are said to represent wisdom that has been acquired through experience. As far as the sitter is concerned, pearls infer that he or she has learned a life lesson recently, having gone through an experience that was probably an unpleasant one. As the saying goes, 'wise after the event'. However, this newly gained wisdom will prepare them for similar future events and allow them to handle it better.

Sea (Ocean)

Symbolises an unsettled time.

Within a reading, the appearance of the sea is designed to make us think about our life. The sitter should consider the vastness and the strength of the sea. It can be calm, but it can suddenly turn violent and unleash its power. For the sitter this can indicate that their life has recently been full of ups and downs, as situations ebb and flow through their recent daily routine. They probably feel as if they have recently been washed about from pillar to post. Calm will return, but they will have to be patient and ride out the storm.

Throne

Symbolises stability.

Within a reading, as a throne is a seat of authority, this represents a position of responsibility for the sitter. Some aspect of the sitter's life is completely under their control. This could be a position at work, as in a managerial post. Possibly at home where the sitter has sole responsibility for raising a child or caring for someone for example. Whichever aspect of the sitter's life the throne refers to, it is running smoothly, but only because of the sitter's determination and steady hand.

49 The King of Cups

Boat (Ship)

Symbolises moving away from past events.

Within a reading, any boat or ship that appears in the spread represents moving on for the sitter. This could signify moving away from emotional troubles. It can also represent that the sitter has, or is about to move onto a new path, or different direction in life.

Crown

Symbolises authority and power.

Within a reading, the appearance of a crown can signify many things. It could suggest that the sitter needs authority in their life. Possibly that the sitter desires recognition for their achievements. Or even that the sitter desires more control of their life, which might feel a little out of control to them at the moment.

Dolphin

Symbolises friends, happiness and amusement.

Within a reading, the appearance of a dolphin represents that the sitter is enjoying a good social life at the moment. It can also represent that the sitter is exploring and enjoying the playful side of their nature.

Goblet/Chalice

Symbolises family and tradition.

Within a reading, the appearance of a goblet or chalice indicates that family is extremely important to the sitter. It implies that the sitter probably possesses a pretty traditional view of what family life means to them. In particular, children and grandchildren mean everything to them and are their very reason for being.

Nautilus Shells

Symbolises renewal.

Within a reading, it should be understood that the nautilus shell grows throughout its life, constantly adding new and larger chambers as it grows. For the sitter, this is a symbol that represents a period of expansion and renewal in some aspect of their life.

Pillar

Symbolises stability.

Within a reading, a pillar or pillars, represent strength, stability and balance. A single pillar can suggest that the sitter is the one who is supporting those around them, as in 'a pillar of strength'. When two pillars appear, usually at each side of the card, this could indicate that the sitter should consider their problems in a more diplomatic, or balanced way. Rather than left or right or black and white, the sitter should try to consider a more central view. In other words, the sitter should adopt a new perspective, a middle-of-the-road approach when tackling their problems.

Pool

Symbolises a fresh start.

Within a reading, a pool can indicate a desire on the sitter's part to 'cleanse' themselves, or to rid themselves of negative thoughts or emotions. The sitter needs to 'wash away' events of their recent past, so that they can restart their life and move on.

Sea (Ocean)

Symbolises an unsettled time.

Within a reading, the appearance of the sea is designed to make us think about our life. The sitter should consider the vastness and the strength of the sea. It can be calm, but it can suddenly turn violent and unleash its power. For the sitter this can indicate that their life has recently been full of ups and downs, as situations ebb and flow through their recent daily routine. They probably feel as if they have recently been washed about from pillar to post. Calm will return, but they will have to be patient and ride out the storm.

Sea Horses

Symbolises grounding.

Within a reading, seahorses are beautiful, serene and graceful creatures. They make no attempt whatsoever to change themselves in order to adapt to their environment. In bad weather they simply curl their tail around something, staying where they are until the bad weather has passed. For the sitter this has the symbolic meaning of 'staying true to yourself'. It can also indicate that the sitter is one of those people who takes whatever life throws at them in their stride.

Shells

Symbolises protection.

Within a reading, the appearance of any kind of shell can infer that the sitter is feeling a little vulnerable at the moment. This could be an emotional, financial or an employment situation that is causing the sitter worry. Whatever is causing trouble for the sitter, he or she needs to prepare for this situation and put a defensive barrier in place, a 'protective shell' to fend off whatever is happening to them at the moment, or for whatever is coming their way.

Throne

Symbolises stability.

Within a reading, as a throne is a seat of authority, this represents a position of responsibility for the sitter. Some aspect of the sitter's life is completely under their control. This could be a position at work, as in a managerial post. Possibly at home where the sitter has sole responsibility for raising a child or caring for someone for example. Whichever aspect of the sitter's life the throne refers to, it is running smoothly, but only because of the sitter's determination and steady hand.

Trees

Symbolises growth.

Within a reading, trees appear in many of the Tarot Cards, but significantly, they usually appear in the background. If trees appear in a lot of the cards within a spread, then this indicates that the sitter has plans for a new venture, path or phase in their life. However, at the moment, these plans are at the back of the sitter's mind. These plans are something that the sitter is considering putting into action in the near future, as they are still working on them, costing them out or carrying out research.

Water

Symbolises cleansing.

Within a reading, water usually represents the need for the sitter to 'cleanse' themselves. Not in the physical sense of needing a wash, but in an emotional or spiritual sense. In other words, the sitter needs to 'wash away' whatever it is that is troubling them. This would normally be an old memory, experience or episode in their life that is holding the sitter back. Once they have removed the issues that are bothering them, they will feel reborn and ready to move on with their life.

50 The Ace of Pentacles / Coins / Discs

Acorns

Symbolises life, fertility and regeneration.

Within a reading, an acorn can indicate that the sitter is undergoing a new phase in their life. They are possibly about to enter a new phase of personal growth. This could be within their personal or professional life. The acorn can represent the germination of a new idea that can only grow stronger.

Bee

Symbolises personal industry or hard work.

Within a reading, a bee represents that the sitter is leading an incredibly busy life. Probably juggling commitments with work, home, children and relationships. While the sitter might well thrive in this environment, it is wise to state the importance of taking time to relax as well.

Clouds

Symbolises transition.

Within a reading, clouds have different meanings depending on what colour they are. In the suit of Swords, most of the clouds are dark and fast moving, representing that the sitter is probably going through a troublesome (or stormy) period in their life. However, dark clouds like these can also represent confusion, or clouded judgement.

Dragon

Symbolises wisdom, strength and courage.

Within a reading, the appearance of a dragon in the spread represents that the sitter needs to rise over their present circumstances in order to see things more clearly. Whatever their currant problem is, they need moral strength and personal courage to overcome it.

Flowers

Symbolises new life and regeneration.

Within a reading, different individual flowers have different meanings. However, flowers in general represent that the sitter is opening (or has already opened) themselves up to new ideas, beliefs or experiences, all of which they will benefit from.

Hand

Symbolises transmission or give and take.

Within a reading, a hand or a pair of hands on their own implies that the sitter should understand that the problem that they are dealing with at this moment in their life, can only be solved with some kind of compromise. Hands give and receive, or give and take, so should the sitter.

Hedgehog

Symbolises rebirth.

Within a reading, because the hedgehog hibernates during the winter and re-emerges in the spring, it is universally regarded as a symbol of rebirth or renewal. For the sitter, this represents a new and busy phase in their life, possibly the awakening of a talent that the sitter was unaware that they had.

Ladybird (Ladybug)

Symbolises good fortune

Within a reading, the appearance of a ladybird recommends that the sitter should try to stop their negative thoughts and concentrate on the things that fill their heart with joy. Also, the ladybird is a symbol of good luck, so possibly the sitter's future might take a turn for the better.

Lilies

Symbolises purity, love and relationships.

Within a reading, the appearance of a lily, or lilies, refers to a period of personal growth and development for the sitter. The lily can also indicate that the sitter (or someone that they are close to) is about to embark on a new relationship or that there is a birth in their immediate future.

Path (Road)

Symbolises life choices.

Within a reading, a path or a road refers to the fact that the sitter is facing a new path in life. The sitter might be about to set out on that new path, or may already have taken their first few steps on it. Either way, this path represents a whole new and potentially exciting future for the sitter. If they are having any doubts about this new path, they shouldn’t worry, as it will be the right choice for them.

51 The Two of Pentacles / Coins / Discs

Bicycle (Bike)

A bicycle symbolises progress.

Within a reading, a bicycle represents the sitter's motivation and determination to proceed with their plans for the future. It is a symbol of progress and promising times ahead.

Boat (Ship)

Symbolises moving away from past events.

Within a reading, any boat or ship that appears in the spread represents moving on for the sitter. This could signify moving away from emotional troubles. It can also represent that the sitter has, or is about to move onto a new path, or different direction in life.

Infinity Symbol

Symbolises endless possibilities.

Within a reading, the Infinity Symbol (The Lemniscate) represents the never-ending possibilities in our lives. For the sitter, it implies that they possess the necessary endless energy to face whatever life throws at them. It can also represent everlasting love.

Sea (Ocean)

Symbolises an unsettled time.

Within a reading, the appearance of the sea is designed to make us think about our life. The sitter should consider the vastness and the strength of the sea. It can be calm, but it can suddenly turn violent and unleash its power. For the sitter this can indicate that their life has recently been full of ups and downs, as situations ebb and flow through their recent daily routine. They probably feel as if they have recently been washed about from pillar to post. Calm will return, but they will have to be patient and ride out the storm.

Water

Symbolises cleansing.

Within a reading, water usually represents the need for the sitter to 'cleanse' themselves. Not in the physical sense of needing a wash, but in an emotional or spiritual sense. In other words, the sitter needs to 'wash away' whatever it is that is troubling them.

This would normally be an old memory, experience or episode in their life that is holding the sitter back. Once they have removed the issues that are bothering them, they will feel reborn and ready to move on with their life.

52 The Three of Pentacles / Coins / Discs

Arch

Symbolises new beginnings.

Within a reading, the arch suggests that the sitter is about to take a new direction in life – whether they know it or not. A new opportunity is about to present itself to the sitter. This could be a new opening at work, a new career path for them to follow or possibly a new romantic involvement.

Bench

Symbolises the need to study the details.

Within a reading, a bench represents the need for the sitter to take their time and to examine the details of the situation that they currently find themselves in. Symbolically 'laying out the plans' and studying them.

Hammer

Symbolises getting a job done.

Within a reading, the appearance of a hammer refers to the fact that the sitter is trying to get a point across, or that the sitter is trying to get a job done, but trying to ensure that it is done properly. It can also suggest that the sitter needs to 'hammer out' the details regarding their work or a project that they are involved in.

Pillar

Symbolises stability.

Within a reading, a pillar or pillars, represent strength, stability and balance. A single pillar can suggest that the sitter is the one who is supporting those around them, as in 'a pillar of strength'. When two pillars appear, usually at each side of the card, this could indicate that the sitter should consider their problems in a more diplomatic, or balanced way. Rather than left or right or black and white, the sitter should try to consider a more central view. In other words, the sitter should adopt a new perspective, a middle-of-the-road approach when tackling their problems.

Shelves

Symbolises storing knowledge.

Within a reading, a shelf or shelves represents the fact that the sitter is facing a decision, but that they are unprepared to make that decision. The shelves are empty at the moment and it is up to the sitter to carry out the necessary research and to acquire the information and the knowledge that they need to fill those shelves. This is the only way that the sitter can face that decision and settle on the correct outcome. Otherwise, the sitter runs the risk of getting it all wrong.

Star (Stars)

Symbolises guidance.

Within a reading, the appearance of stars in the spread indicates that the sitter is experiencing some turmoil in their life at the moment. Their life seems to be a little topsy-turvy right now, causing them a lot of confusion. The star symbol deals with shedding some light into their life. They must focus on one problem at a time and deal with it, moving onto the next problem and dealing with that and so on. There is light at the end of the tunnel, but the illumination of that light comes from within.

Tools

Symbolises reshaping your life.

Within a reading, the appearance of one, or a collection of tools is an indication that the sitter is doing something wrong. Whatever path that the sitter is following is either the wrong path for them, or that they are following the correct path incorrectly. The time has come for the sitter to gather the tools that they need (possibly tools that they have never considered before) in order to 'reshape' their path in life. In this case, the tools that the sitter needs are information, research and a lot of soul searching.

Window

Symbolises a new outlook.

Within a reading, a window represents a new perspective, or a new opportunity. However, it can also indicate that the sitter feels as if they are on the outside looking in. The time has come for the sitter to move inside and take an active part in whatever it is that they have been observing. Only by joining in will they be able to take advantage of all the new opportunities that will be within their grasp.

53 The Four of Pentacles / Coins / Discs

Arch

Symbolises new beginnings.

Within a reading, the arch suggests that the sitter is about to take a new direction in life – whether they know it or not. A new opportunity is about to present itself to the sitter. This could be a new opening at work, a new career path for them to follow or possibly a new romantic involvement.

Buckle (Silver)

Symbolises loyalty and trustworthiness.

Within a reading, a buckle can represent the sitter's need to 'buckle down' and get on with it. Whenever we use a buckle, we depend on it doing its job. In the same sense, a buckle can denote the sitter's sense of loyalty, trustworthiness and possibly even dependency.

Castle

Symbolises goals and achievements.

Within a reading, a castle represents the sitter's long and difficult journey to achieve their goal in life. This might be a long university degree course, or a long battle against illness. Whatever the sitter's goal is, they are well on their way to achieving it. On a simpler note, a castle can represent security or sanctuary.

City / Village

Symbolises protection, harmony and teamwork.

Within a reading, a city, town or village appearing in the spread represents a place where people gather. Whatever the sitter is trying to do in life, they cannot do it alone. A group effort is required and the sitter should try and find the group that they need in order to accomplish their goals.

Crown

Symbolises authority and power.

Within a reading, the appearance of a crown can signify many things. It could suggest that the sitter needs authority in their life. Possibly that the sitter desires recognition for their achievements. Or even that the sitter desires more control of their life, which might feel a little out of control to them at the moment.

Door (Portal)

Symbolises the opening to a new path in life.

Within a reading, any door of any shape, size or colour represents that the sitter is about to open that door and start out on a new path in life. Of course, this door may well have just opened for the sitter and they have already begun their journey.

Flagstones

Symbolises a solid base or foundations.

Within a reading, flagstones can represent the sitter's need, or possibly their search for stability in life. This could manifest itself as the sitter's search for a job, somewhere to live or a stable relationship.

54 The Five of Pentacles / Coins / Discs

Arch

Symbolises new beginnings.

Within a reading, the arch suggests that the sitter is about to take a new direction in life – whether they know it or not. A new opportunity is about to present itself to the sitter. This could be a new opening at work, a new career path for them to follow or possibly a new romantic involvement.

Begging Bowl

Symbolises the need of help from some quarter.

Within a reading, a begging bowl can represent the sitter needing and asking for help and assistance with some aspect of their life. By contrast, a begging bowl can also represent that the sitter is a generous giver of their time to help others.

Crutch

Symbolises physical and spiritual support.

Within a reading, the appearance of a crutch represents the fact that the sitter is in need of some kind of support. As a rule, this is more likely to be some kind of emotional support. However, it can also represent the sitter's need for financial support, or support from colleagues at work.

Door (Portal)

Symbolises the opening to a new path in life.

Within a reading, any door of any shape, size or colour represents that the sitter is about to open that door and start out on a new path in life. Of course, this door may well have just opened for the sitter and they have already begun their journey.

Snow (Snowflakes)

Symbolises a fresh start.

Within a reading, snow can have two interpretations. In the first instance, the sitter might be feeling that some important information is being kept from them. They might feel that they are getting the 'cold shoulder' or that they are being 'kept out in the cold' because something is being withheld. On the other hand, a blanket of snow can represent a fresh start, a whole new beginning, as the blanket of snow gives promise of the springtime to come.

Stained Glass

Symbolises your outlook.

Within a reading, when stained glass appears in the spread, it is often regarded as the spiritual window to the soul. For the sitter however, it is a sign that the time has come to start being honest with themselves about a situation that is unfolding around them. They must ask themselves if they are looking at this situation clearly, or are they looking at it through 'rose coloured glasses'?

Window

Symbolises a new outlook.

Within a reading, a window represents a new perspective, or a new opportunity. However, it can also indicate that the sitter feels as if they are on the outside looking in. The time has come for the sitter to move inside and take an active part in whatever it is that they have been observing. Only by joining in will they be able to take advantage of all the new opportunities that will be within their grasp.

55 The Six of Pentacles / Coins / Discs

Begging Bowl

Symbolises the need of help from some quarter.

Within a reading, a begging bowl can represent the sitter needing and asking for help and assistance with some aspect of their life. By contrast, a begging bowl can also represent that the sitter is a generous giver of their time to help others.

Chains

Symbolises restraint or restriction.

Within a reading, chains represent that the sitter is feeling held back, or being prevented from carrying out some action or other. If the chains are presented as some form of jewellery, then the sitter's problem is of a more delicate nature.

Child/Children

Symbolises innocence and memories.

Within a reading, a child or children appearing in the spread signifies that the sitter might be living in the past too much. Childhood memories can be happy or sad, but should never be dwelled upon. However, children in the tarot can also represent promise for the future, or the beginning of a new venture, as well as a child-like enthusiasm for life.

Feathers

Symbolises spiritual evolution.

Within a reading, a feather (or feathers) represents that the sitter is becoming aware of their spiritual side and that they are probably keen to advance that interest. Within the spiritual movement, feathers are universally recognised as a sign from Spirit, or a loved one that has passed.

Scales

Symbolises balance.

Within a reading, scales have the fairly obvious meaning of balance. For the sitter however, the scales can represent that some aspect of their life is actually out of balance. Something in their life is throwing them out of kilter, so the sitter needs to identify the cause of this imbalance and take the required action in order to restore the equilibrium.

56 The Seven of Pentacles / Coins / Discs

Grapes (Grapevines)

Symbolises bountifulness.

Within a reading, grapes or grapevines imply that the sitter is a very hospitable and generous person, who enjoys sharing the fruits of their bounty (work or good fortune) with others. Can also signify abundance and fertility within the sitter's life.

Hoe

Symbolises resourcefulness.

Within a reading, the hoe (or any other tool) suggests that the sitter can make their present path a lot easier to negotiate if they use the resources (the tools) that they have available to them. In other words, should the sitter carry on doing things the hard way, or is it time to ask for some help?

Red Sky

Symbolises trouble ahead.

Within a reading, the red sky is not telling the sitter that tomorrow will be a nice day as the old saying goes. It appears in the spread as a warning of trouble ahead. The sitter may not know what this warning refers to, but now is the time for the sitter to anticipate the probable problem, or problems that are coming their way and to prepare for it.

Wheat

Symbolises abundance.

Within a reading, the appearance of wheat indicates a period of growth, renewal and abundance. A wheat field is a thing of beauty to behold, conjuring up images of golden summers and happy childhood memories. For the sitter, this implies that they have entered, or are about to enter a 'golden' phase in their life. All of the sitter's hard work, planning and/or patience is about to be rewarded.

57 The Eight of Pentacles / Coins / Discs

Bench

Symbolises the need to study the details.

Within a reading, a bench represents the need for the sitter to take their time and to examine the details of the situation that they currently find themselves in. Symbolically 'laying out the plans' and studying them.

Blueprints

Symbolises the necessity of studying the details.

Within a reading, a blueprint represents that the sitter really needs to examine all of the details before committing themselves to some plan or relationship. It can also represent the fact that the sitter is going through some changes in their life.

Castle

Symbolises goals and achievements.

Within a reading, a castle represents the sitter's long and difficult journey to achieve their goal in life. This might be a long university degree course, or a long battle against illness. Whatever the sitter's goal is, they are well on their way to achieving it. On a simpler note, a castle can represent security or sanctuary.

Hammer

Symbolises getting a job done.

Within a reading, the appearance of a hammer refers to the fact that the sitter is trying to get a point across, or that the sitter is trying to get a job done, but trying to ensure that it is done properly. It can also suggest that the sitter needs to 'hammer out' the details regarding their work or a project that they are involved in.

Tools

Symbolises reshaping your life.

Within a reading, the appearance of one, or a collection of tools is an indication that the sitter is doing something wrong. Whatever path that the sitter is following is either the wrong path for them, or that they are following the correct path incorrectly. The time has come for the sitter to gather the tools that they need (possibly tools that they have never considered before) in order to 'reshape' their path in life. In this case, the tools that the sitter needs are information, research and a lot of soul searching.

Window

Symbolises a new outlook.

Within a reading, a window represents a new perspective, or a new opportunity. However, it can also indicate that the sitter feels as if they are on the outside looking in. The time has come for the sitter to move inside and take an active part in whatever it is that they have been observing. Only by joining in will they be able to take advantage of all the new opportunities that will be within their grasp.

Workbench

Symbolises creativity.

Within a reading, the appearance of a workbench indicates that the sitter is going through a busy time right now, or is possibly just about to begin a busy period in their life. The workbench hints at hard work, industrious efforts and creativity. The sitter must work hard to achieve the goals that they have set for themselves, but this is not an issue for them. They are ready, willing and able with all of the tools that they need at hand, in order to achieve that goal.

58 The Nine of Pentacles / Coins / Discs

Arch

Symbolises new beginnings.

Within a reading, the arch suggests that the sitter is about to take a new direction in life – whether they know it or not. A new opportunity is about to present itself to the sitter. This could be a new opening at work, a new career path for them to follow or possibly a new romantic involvement.

Bird of Paradise

Symbolises the appreciation of beauty.

Within a reading, the bird of paradise represents the sitter's love and appreciation of all things beautiful. This could be art, nature or even surrounding themselves with beautiful objects, furniture or even clothes.

Castle

Symbolises goals and achievements.

Within a reading, a castle represents the sitter's long and difficult journey to achieve their goal in life. This might be a long university degree course, or a long battle against illness. Whatever the sitter's goal is, they are well on their way to achieving it. On a simpler note, a castle can represent security or sanctuary.

Flowers

Symbolises new life and regeneration.

Within a reading, different individual flowers have different meanings. However, flowers in general represent that the sitter is opening (or has already opened) themselves up to new ideas, beliefs or experiences, all of which they will benefit from.

Grapes (Grapevines)

Symbolises bountifulness.

Within a reading, grapes or grapevines imply that the sitter is a very hospitable and generous person, who enjoys sharing the fruits of their bounty (work or good fortune) with others. Can also signify abundance and fertility within the sitter's life.

Pool

Symbolises a fresh start.

Within a reading, a pool can indicate a desire on the sitter's part to 'cleanse' themselves, or to rid themselves of negative thoughts or emotions. The sitter needs to 'wash away' events of their recent past, so that they can restart their life and move on.

Snail

Symbolises steady progress.

Within a reading, a snail indicates that the sitter might be trying to rush things. Whatever goal that the sitter is aiming to achieve, they should realise that there is no shortcut. No matter how hard the sitter tries, their progress cannot be hurried. Success does not come overnight, but it will happen. The snail represents slow, but steady progress and the sitter will just have to learn to be a bit less impatient.

Trees

Symbolises growth.

Within a reading, trees appear in many of the Tarot Cards, but significantly, they usually appear in the background. If trees appear in a lot of the cards within a spread, then this indicates that the sitter has plans for a new venture, path or phase in their life. However, at the moment, these plans are at the back of the sitter's mind. These plans are something that the sitter is considering putting into action in the near future, as they are still working on them, costing them out or carrying out research.

59 The Ten of Pentacles / Coins / Discs

Arch

Symbolises new beginnings.

Within a reading, the arch suggests that the sitter is about to take a new direction in life – whether they know it or not. A new opportunity is about to present itself to the sitter. This could be a new opening at work, a new career path for them to follow or possibly a new romantic involvement.

Castle

Symbolises goals and achievements.

Within a reading, a castle represents the sitter's long and difficult journey to achieve their goal in life. This might be a long university degree course, or a long battle against illness. Whatever the sitter's goal is, they are well on their way to achieving it. On a simpler note, a castle can represent security or sanctuary.

Chains

Symbolises restraint or restriction.

Within a reading, chains represent that the sitter is feeling held back, or being prevented from carrying out some action or other. If the chains are presented as some form of jewellery, then the sitter's problem is of a more delicate nature.

Child/Children

Symbolises innocence and memories.

Within a reading, a child or children appearing in the spread signifies that the sitter might be living in the past too much. Childhood memories can be happy or sad, but should never be dwelled upon. However, children in the tarot can also represent promise for the future, or the beginning of a new venture, as well as a child-like enthusiasm for life.

City / Village

Symbolises protection, harmony and teamwork.

Within a reading, a city, town or village appearing in the spread represents a place where people gather. Whatever the sitter is trying to do in life, they cannot do it alone. A group effort is required and the sitter should try and find the group that they need in order to accomplish their goals.

Dog/Dogs

Symbolises loyalty or devotion.

Within a reading, whenever a dog (or dogs) appear in the spread it represents that the sitter might be experiencing loyalty issues. However, a dog can also represent that the sitter is on the right track in life, as dogs are symbolic of stability and steadfastness.

Grapes (Grapevines)

Symbolises bountifulness.

Within a reading, grapes or grapevines imply that the sitter is a very hospitable and generous person, who enjoys sharing the fruits of their bounty (work or good fortune) with others. Can also signify abundance and fertility within the sitter's life.

Key

Symbolises unlocking potential.

Within a reading, a key usually represents the fact that the sitter is about to unlock a hidden talent, or that they are about to open a new door (new path) in their life. Depending on the sitter's circumstances, a key can also represent closing a door on some part of their life, as in something coming to an end for the sitter.

Treasure Box

Symbolises secrets.

Within a reading, a treasure box implies that the sitter is keeping something to themselves. This could be a memory of something that has happened to the sitter that they wish to keep secret. It could be information about someone or something that they have been entrusted with and that they know they must never reveal. If this is a sentimental memory, then they should keep it close to their heart and cherish it. On the other hand, if this memory relates to something nasty that has happened, then now is the time to seek help.

60 The Page of Pentacles / Coins / Discs

Flowers

Symbolises new life and regeneration.

Within a reading, different individual flowers have different meanings. However, flowers in general represent that the sitter is opening (or has already opened) themselves up to new ideas, beliefs or experiences, all of which they will benefit from.

Hills

Symbolises obstacles.

Within a reading, the appearance of hills in the spread suggests that the sitter is facing obstacles in their life that they need to overcome. However daunting or impossible these hurdles might appear to be for the sitter, they need to remove these obstacles in their life in order to move on.

Mountains

Symbolises challenges.

Within a reading, mountains usually appear in the background of the card. For the sitter, this suggests that they are facing seemingly insurmountable challenges, but that the sitter is trying to ignore them, pushing them to the back of their mind. If mountains appear in the majority of the spread, this indicates that the time has come for the sitter to face those challenges and to deal with them.

Ploughed Fields

Symbolises care and planning.

Within a reading, ploughed fields remind the sitter that 'we reap what we sew'. The sitter must keep in mind that whatever they do today will ultimately affect their future plans and outcomes. The sitter will benefit from a bit of careful thought and planning before they start any new venture. It would be helpful if the sitter remembers that ploughed fields can also represent time. Just as it takes time for crops to grow, so it takes time for our plans to come to fruition, so the sitter must try and understand that patience will be required.

Trees

Symbolises growth.

Within a reading, trees appear in many of the Tarot Cards, but significantly, they usually appear in the background. If trees appear in a lot of the cards within a spread, then this indicates that the sitter has plans for a new venture, path or phase in their life. However, at the moment, these plans are at the back of the sitter's mind. These plans are something that the sitter is considering putting into action in the near future, as they are still working on them, costing them out or carrying out research.

61 The Knight of Pentacles / Coins / Discs

Armour

Symbolises protection and strength.

Within a reading, the appearance of armour suggests that the sitter is feeling vulnerable in some way and that they feel the need to protect themselves from their perceived threat.

Helmet

Symbolises protection.

Within a reading, a helmet can suggest that the sitter is feeling vulnerable in some way and is looking for a way to protect themselves from the cause. Usually a helmet has a plume or crest on top of it for identification. This could suggest that the sitter is searching for acceptance in some way.

Horns

Symbolises physical prowess.

Within a reading, the appearance of horns indicates that the sitter is experiencing (or is in need of) fighting spirit in order to overcome a challenge that they are currently facing. It can also infer that the sitter has to take this challenge head on (by the horns), as there is really no other way of dealing with it.

Horse

Symbolises strength and freedom.

Within a reading, a horse refers to the sitter's personal drive and a desire to free themselves from the current path that they are following. The sitter has the strength and stamina to easily achieve this goal, but they have to believe in themselves. Horses are also regarded as a deep spiritual sign, which might hint at the sitter's need for some spiritual guidance. Maybe the sitter needs to free themselves from old beliefs.

Path (Road)

Symbolises life choices.

Within a reading, a path or a road refers to the fact that the sitter is facing a new path in life. The sitter might be about to set out on that new path, or may already have taken their first few steps on it. Either way, this path represents a whole new and potentially exciting future for the sitter. If they are having any doubts about this new path, they shouldn't worry, as it will be the right choice for them.

Ploughed Fields

Symbolises care and planning.

Within a reading, ploughed fields remind the sitter that 'we reap what we sew'. The sitter must keep in mind that whatever they do today will ultimately affect their future plans and outcomes. The sitter will benefit from a bit of careful thought and planning before they start any new venture. It would be helpful if the sitter remembers that ploughed fields can also represent time. Just as it takes time for crops to grow, so it takes time for our plans to come to fruition, so the sitter must try and understand that patience will be required.

Trees

Symbolises growth.

Within a reading, trees appear in many of the Tarot Cards, but significantly, they usually appear in the background. If trees appear in a lot of the cards within a spread, then this indicates that the sitter has plans for a new venture, path or phase in their life. However, at the moment, these plans are at the back of the sitter's mind. These plans are something that the sitter is considering putting into action in the near future, as they are still working on them, costing them out or carrying out research.

62 The Queen of Pentacles / Coins / Discs

Chains

Symbolises restraint or restriction.

Within a reading, chains represent that the sitter is feeling held back, or being prevented from carrying out some action or other. If the chains are presented as some form of jewellery, then the sitter's problem is of a more delicate nature.

Crown

Symbolises authority and power.

Within a reading, the appearance of a crown can signify many things. It could suggest that the sitter needs authority in their life. Possibly that the sitter desires recognition for their achievements. Or even that the sitter desires more control of their life, which might feel a little out of control to them at the moment.

Flowers

Symbolises new life and regeneration.

Within a reading, different individual flowers have different meanings. However, flowers in general represent that the sitter is opening (or has already opened) themselves up to new ideas, beliefs or experiences, all of which they will benefit from.

Mountains

Symbolises challenges.

Within a reading, mountains usually appear in the background of the card. For the sitter, this suggests that they are facing seemingly insurmountable challenges, but that the sitter is trying to ignore them, pushing them to the back of their mind. If mountains appear in the majority of the spread, this indicates that the time has come for the sitter to face those challenges and to deal with them.

Rabbit

Symbolises being grounded.

Within a reading, rabbits are considered to be a strong spiritual symbol in the world of spiritualism. It can be regarded as a sign that the sitter is beginning to, or has already started to understand their spiritual needs, as opposed to their materialistic needs. This is probably manifesting itself in the sitters mind as understanding the importance of family and friends, for it is the people who are closest to us that keep us grounded in the real world.

Ram

Symbolises determination.

Within a reading, the appearance of a ram, or a ram's head indicates that the time has come for the sitter to take action and get themselves motivated in order to accomplish their goals. Whatever their goal in life is, it is not going to come along and drop itself in their lap. They must take responsibility, get up, get out there and start the process by themselves.

Roses

Symbolises balance.

Within a reading, a rose, or roses, have always been associated with love, affection and relationships. For the sitter, they should remember that the rose represents promise and new beginnings. However, the sitter should be aware of the fact that the rose also has thorns. The thorns can represent possible painful ordeals along the way. As beautiful as a rose is, there is a balance to be struck.

Throne

Symbolises stability.

Within a reading, as a throne is a seat of authority, this represents a position of responsibility for the sitter. Some aspect of the sitter's life is completely under their control. This could be a position at work, as in a managerial post. Possibly at home where the sitter has sole responsibility for raising a child or caring for someone for example. Whichever aspect of the sitter's life the throne refers to, it is running smoothly, but only because of the sitter's determination and steady hand.

63 The King of Pentacles / Coins / Discs

Balcony

Symbolises an elevated position that gives you a different perspective.

Within a reading, a balcony represents the sitter's need to raise themselves above it all and to look at things differently. This detached view of their life and/or problems will help them to see things more clearly.

Bull

Symbolises power and stability.

Within a reading, the appearance of a bull can represent quite a few things for the sitter. It could point to the sitter's resistance to change, as in being 'bull headed'. However, it can also suggest to the sitter that the time has come to stand their ground and fight for what they believe in.

Castle

Symbolises goals and achievements.

Within a reading, a castle represents the sitter's long and difficult journey to achieve their goal in life. This might be a long university degree course, or a long battle against illness. Whatever the sitter's goal is, they are well on their way to achieving it. On a simpler note, a castle can represent security or sanctuary.

Crown

Symbolises authority and power.

Within a reading, the appearance of a crown can signify many things. It could suggest that the sitter needs authority in their life. Possibly that the sitter desires recognition for their achievements. Or even that the sitter desires more control of their life, which might feel a little out of control to them at the moment.

Grapes (Grapevines)

Symbolises bountifulness.

Within a reading, grapes or grapevines imply that the sitter is a very hospitable and generous person, who enjoys sharing the fruits of their bounty (work or good fortune) with others. Can also signify abundance and fertility within the sitter's life.

Pillar

Symbolises stability.

Within a reading, a pillar or pillars, represent strength, stability and balance. A single pillar can suggest that the sitter is the one who is supporting those around them, as in 'a pillar of strength'. When two pillars appear, usually at each side of the card, this could indicate that the sitter should consider their problems in a more diplomatic, or balanced way. Rather than left or right or black and white, the sitter should try to consider a more central view. In other words, the sitter should adopt a new perspective, a middle-of-the-road approach when tackling their problems.

Throne

Symbolises stability.

Within a reading, as a throne is a seat of authority, this represents a position of responsibility for the sitter. Some aspect of the sitter's life is completely under their control. This could be a position at work, as in a managerial post. Possibly at home where the sitter has sole responsibility for raising a child or caring for someone for example. Whichever aspect of the sitter's life the throne refers to, it is running smoothly, but only because of the sitter's determination and steady hand.

Wall

Symbolises barriers.

Within a reading, a wall represents building a barrier in life. For the sitter, this refers to them needing to separate one area of their life from another. The surrounding cards should give an indication as to what areas need separating. It can also suggest that the sitter is holding back in some way, hiding behind a wall of their own making. However, a wall can also suggest quite simply that the sitter is in need of some privacy.

64 The Ace of Wands / Rods

Castle

Symbolises goals and achievements.

Within a reading, a castle represents the sitter's long and difficult journey to achieve their goal in life. This might be a long university degree course, or a long battle against illness. Whatever the sitter's goal is, they are well on their way to achieving it. On a simpler note, a castle can represent security or sanctuary.

Clouds

Symbolises transition.

Within a reading, clouds have different meanings depending on what colour they are. In the suit of Swords, most of the clouds are dark and fast moving, representing that the sitter is probably going through a troublesome (or stormy) period in their life. However, dark clouds like these can also represent confusion, or clouded judgement.

Dragon

Symbolises wisdom, strength and courage.

Within a reading, the appearance of a dragon in the spread represents that the sitter needs to rise over their present circumstances in order to see things more clearly. Whatever their currant problem is, they need moral strength and personal courage to overcome it.

Fire (Flames)

Symbolises transformation.

Within a reading, fire or flames represents that the sitter is going through some kind of transition in their life. They can also represent that the sitter might need to make some kind of change, alteration or modification to their lifestyle.

Hand

Symbolises transmission or give and take.

Within a reading, a hand or a pair of hands on their own implies that the sitter should understand that the problem that they are dealing with at this moment in their life, can only be solved with some kind of compromise. Hands give and receive, or give and take, so should the sitter.

Lilies

Symbolises purity, love and relationships.

Within a reading, the appearance of a lily, or lilies, refers to a period of personal growth and development for the sitter. The lily can also indicate that the sitter (or someone that they are close to) is about to embark on a new relationship or that there is a birth in their immediate future.

Mountains

Symbolises challenges.

Within a reading, mountains usually appear in the background of the card. For the sitter, this suggests that they are facing seemingly insurmountable challenges, but that the sitter is trying to ignore them, pushing them to the back of their mind. If mountains appear in the majority of the spread, this indicates that the time has come for the sitter to face those challenges and to deal with them.

Sunrise

Symbolises a new beginning.

Within a reading, the image of a sunrise, or dawn, infers that the sitter is about to enter a new phase in their life. This could be the beginning of a new venture, a new project or possibly even the start of a new relationship. It also heralds a real chance for happiness, so the sitter should embrace this new start just as they would embrace a new day.

Trees

Symbolises growth.

Within a reading, trees appear in many of the Tarot Cards, but significantly, they usually appear in the background. If trees appear in a lot of the cards within a spread, then this indicates that the sitter has plans for a new venture, path or phase in their life. However, at the moment, these plans are at the back of the sitter's mind. These plans are something that the sitter is considering putting into action in the near future, as they are still working on them, costing them out or carrying out research.

65 The Two of Wands / Rods

Flowers

Symbolises new life and regeneration.

Within a reading, different individual flowers have different meanings. However, flowers in general represent that the sitter is opening (or has already opened) themselves up to new ideas, beliefs or experiences, all of which they will benefit from.

Globe

Symbolises achievement.

Within a reading, globes are sometimes shown as crystal balls or as the world, both of which are round in shape. Any round object or circle represents completion. This refers to the fact that the sitter is about to achieve some goal in their life. It is a sign of completion and infers that the sitter has the 'world at their fingertips'.

Key

Symbolises unlocking potential.

Within a reading, a key usually represents the fact that the sitter is about to unlock a hidden talent, or that they are about to open a new door (new path) in their life. Depending on the sitter's circumstances, a key can also represent closing a door on some part of their life, as in something coming to an end for the sitter.

Mountains

Symbolises challenges.

Within a reading, mountains usually appear in the background of the card. For the sitter, this suggests that they are facing seemingly insurmountable challenges, but that the sitter is trying to ignore them, pushing them to the back of their mind. If mountains appear in the majority of the spread, this indicates that the time has come for the sitter to face those challenges and to deal with them.

Ribbons

Symbolises fragility.

Within a reading, ribbons should never be ignored, as they bring to our attention just how fragile the bonds that bind us really are. The sitter should take a good look at the relationships that they have with those who are closest to them. Are they treating their loved ones, their friends or colleagues with the respect that they deserve? If not, they could end up forcing then away.

Roses

Symbolises balance.

Within a reading, a rose, or roses, have always been associated with love, affection and relationships. For the sitter, they should remember that the rose represents promise and new beginnings. However, the sitter should be aware of the fact that the rose also has thorns. The thorns can represent possible painful ordeals along the way. As beautiful as a rose is, there is a balance to be struck.

Sea (Ocean)

Symbolises an unsettled time.

Within a reading, the appearance of the sea is designed to make us think about our life. The sitter should consider the vastness and the strength of the sea. It can be calm, but it can suddenly turn violent and unleash its power. For the sitter this can indicate that their life has recently been full of ups and downs, as situations ebb and flow through their recent daily routine. They probably feel as if they have recently been washed about from pillar to post. Calm will return, but they will have to be patient and ride out the storm.

Sunset

Symbolises an ending.

Within a reading, the image of a sunset infers that some aspect of the sitter's life is winding down or coming to an end. This could be a period of intense work, a difficult phase, a troubling time or maybe just the end of a project that has taken longer to complete than anticipated. Whatever it is that is coming to an end, it is now time for the sitter to relax, as the worst is now over.

Treasure Box

Symbolises secrets.

Within a reading, a treasure box implies that the sitter is keeping something to themselves. This could be a memory of something that has happened to the sitter that they wish to keep secret. It could be information about someone or something that they have been entrusted with and that they know they must never reveal. If this is a sentimental memory, then they should keep it close to their heart and cherish it. On the other hand, if this memory relates to something nasty that has happened, then now is the time to seek help.

Wall

Symbolises barriers.

Within a reading, a wall represents building a barrier in life. For the sitter, this refers to them needing to separate one area of their life from another. The surrounding cards should give an indication as to what areas need separating. It can also suggest that the sitter is holding back in some way, hiding behind a wall of their own making. However, a wall can also suggest quite simply that the sitter is in need of some privacy.

66 The Three of Wands / Rods

Airship

Symbolises flying. (Although only present in one card in one deck, I have included this symbol as it represents flying.)

Within a reading, an airship (or flying) indicates that the sitter needs to take a step back and look at their problems from another perspective. Only by changing their point of view will they be able to see a possible solution.

Bird

Any species of bird symbolises rising above the normal.

Within a reading, a bird represents the sitter's need to lighten their thoughts. To rise above the problems of the material world and to look at the bigger picture. A bird can also symbolise the sitter's need to look at and to raise their individual spirituality.

Boat (Ship)

Symbolises moving away from past events.

Within a reading, any boat or ship that appears in the spread represents moving on for the sitter. This could signify moving away from emotional troubles. It can also represent that the sitter has, or is about to move onto a new path, or different direction in life.

Cliff Edge

Signifies possible new opportunities.

Within a reading, a cliff edge can represent two things. The sitter is about to embark on a new path, which has been created by the arrival of a new opportunity in their life. On one hand, this is an exciting time for the sitter. On the other hand, they should take precautions, as there are potential pitfalls ahead.

Sea (Ocean)

Symbolises an unsettled time.

Within a reading, the appearance of the sea is designed to make us think about our life. The sitter should consider the vastness and the strength of the sea. It can be calm, but it can suddenly turn violent and unleash its power. For the sitter this can indicate that their life has recently been full of ups and downs, as situations ebb and flow through their recent daily routine. They probably feel as if they have recently been washed about from pillar to post. Calm will return, but they will have to be patient and ride out the storm.

Sunset

Symbolises an ending.

Within a reading, the image of a sunset infers that some aspect of the sitter's life is winding down or coming to an end. This could be a period of intense work, a difficult phase, a troubling time or maybe just the end of a project that has taken longer to complete than anticipated. Whatever it is that is coming to an end, it is now time for the sitter to relax, as the worst is now over.

67 The Four of Wands / Rods

Arch

Symbolises new beginnings.

Within a reading, the arch suggests that the sitter is about to take a new direction in life – whether they know it or not. A new opportunity is about to present itself to the sitter. This could be a new opening at work, a new career path for them to follow or possibly a new romantic involvement.

Bird

Any species of bird symbolises rising above the normal.

Within a reading, a bird represents the sitter's need to lighten their thoughts. To rise above the problems of the material world and to look at the bigger picture. A bird can also symbolise the sitter's need to look at and to raise their individual spirituality.

Bridge

Symbolises dwelling on the past.

Within a reading, the appearance of a bridge represents the sitter's mind being stuck in past events. The bridge is a reminder to the sitter that it is time to move on to a new phase in their life.

Castle

Symbolises goals and achievements.

Within a reading, a castle represents the sitter's long and difficult journey to achieve their goal in life. This might be a long university degree course, or a long battle against illness. Whatever the sitter's goal is, they are well on their way to achieving it. On a simpler note, a castle can represent security or sanctuary.

Flowers

Symbolises new life and regeneration.

Within a reading, different individual flowers have different meanings. However, flowers in general represent that the sitter is opening (or has already opened) themselves up to new ideas, beliefs or experiences, all of which they will benefit from.

Grapes (Grapevines)

Symbolises bountifulness.

Within a reading, grapes or grapevines imply that the sitter is a very hospitable and generous person, who enjoys sharing the fruits of their bounty (work or good fortune) with others. Can also signify abundance and fertility within the sitter's life.

Moat

Symbolises protection.

Within a reading, a moat suggests that the sitter is feeling vulnerable at the moment. The sitter feels in need of protecting themselves in some aspect of their life, which is probably an emotional issue. A moat can also represent the sitter's need to cut themselves off from something, to stop it in its tracks, possibly the emotional issue mentioned above.

Rainbow

Symbolises success and hope.

Within a reading, the shape of a rainbow can appear to resemble a bridge. This is significant for the sitter, as it implies that he or she has some bridges to build or repair in their life. This could be bridges in their professional or private lives. Now is the time to start, as the basic symbolism of a rainbow is success and joy.

River

Symbolises obstacles.

Within a reading, the appearance of a river can be interpreted in two different ways. For the sitter, a river can represent an obstacle that they have to get across, as it is blocking their path or progress. On the other hand, it could be advising the sitter to stop struggling with whatever problem that they are facing or dealing with. It is time for them to 'go with the flow' and let the problem resolve itself.

Trees

Symbolises growth.

Within a reading, trees appear in many of the Tarot Cards, but significantly, they usually appear in the background. If trees appear in a lot of the cards within a spread, then this indicates that

the sitter has plans for a new venture, path or phase in their life. However, at the moment, these plans are at the back of the sitter's mind. These plans are something that the sitter is considering putting into action in the near future, as they are still working on them, costing them out or carrying out research.

68 The Five of Wands / Rods

Battle

Symbolises conflict or struggle.

Within a reading, a battle scene represents that the sitter is experiencing some kind of struggle in their life. This could be an emotional struggle, or possibly a struggle with a legal procedure.

Dragon

Symbolises wisdom, strength and courage.

Within a reading, the appearance of a dragon in the spread represents that the sitter needs to rise over their present circumstances in order to see things more clearly. Whatever their currant problem is, they need moral strength and personal courage to overcome it.

Gauntlets (Gloves)

Symbolises a challenge.

Within a reading, the appearance of a gauntlet represents that the sitter is facing some kind of challenge in their life, as in 'throwing down the gauntlet'. This could be a challenge that they face, or a challenge that they have made.

Red Sky

Symbolises trouble ahead.

Within a reading, the red sky is not telling the sitter that tomorrow will be a nice day as the old saying goes. It appears in the spread as a warning of trouble ahead. The sitter may not know what this warning refers to, but now is the time for the sitter to anticipate the probable problem, or problems that are coming their way and to prepare for it.

Trees

Symbolises growth.

Within a reading, trees appear in many of the Tarot Cards, but significantly, they usually appear in the background. If trees appear in a lot of the cards within a spread, then this indicates that the sitter has plans for a new venture, path or phase in their life. However, at the moment, these plans are at the back of the sitter's mind. These plans are something that the sitter is considering putting into action in the near future, as they are still working on them, costing them out or carrying out research.

69 The Six of Wands / Rods

Arch

Symbolises new beginnings.

Within a reading, the arch suggests that the sitter is about to take a new direction in life – whether they know it or not. A new opportunity is about to present itself to the sitter. This could be a new opening at work, a new career path for them to follow or possibly a new romantic involvement.

Chains

Symbolises restraint or restriction.

Within a reading, chains represent that the sitter is feeling held back, or being prevented from carrying out some action or other. If the chains are presented as some form of jewellery, then the sitter's problem is of a more delicate nature.

Dragon

Symbolises wisdom, strength and courage.

Within a reading, the appearance of a dragon in the spread represents that the sitter needs to rise over their present circumstances in order to see things more clearly. Whatever their currant problem is, they need moral strength and personal courage to overcome it.

Gauntlets (Gloves)

Symbolises a challenge.

Within a reading, the appearance of a gauntlet represents that the sitter is facing some kind of challenge in their life, as in 'throwing down the gauntlet'. This could be a challenge that they face, or a challenge that they have made.

Helmet

Symbolises protection.

Within a reading, a helmet can suggest that the sitter is feeling vulnerable in some way and is looking for a way to protect themselves from the cause. Usually a helmet has a plume or crest on top of it for identification. This could suggest that the sitter is searching for acceptance in some way.

Horse

Symbolises strength and freedom.

Within a reading, a horse refers to the sitter's personal drive and a desire to free themselves from the current path that they are following. The sitter has the strength and stamina to easily achieve this goal, but they have to believe in themselves. Horses are also regarded as a deep spiritual sign, which might hint at the sitter's need for some spiritual guidance. Maybe the sitter needs to free themselves from old beliefs.

Laurel Wreath

Symbolises achievement.

Within a reading, the appearance of a laurel wreath indicates that the sitter has recently achieved something in their life that they are very proud of. This could be anything from passing an exam, getting the job that they have always wanted or overcoming some personal problem that has been holding them back.

Shield

Symbolises protection.

Within a reading, the appearance of a shield represents that the sitter is in need of protecting themselves and those that they love from the harsh realities of life. No matter how happy, safe and secure they might feel at the moment, they should be deeply aware that they are as vulnerable as the rest of us. However, being aware of this vulnerability will allow them to prepare themselves in order to be ready to raise their protective shield whenever they need it.

Sun

Symbolises life and rebirth.

Within a reading, just as the sun rises every morning, so a new day begins for the sitter. The position of the sun in a Tarot card is also significant. A rising sun promises new beginnings, while a setting sun infers that something is coming to an end. A full mid-day sun indicates energy, strength and success in creative endeavours.

Triangle

Symbolises strength.

Within a reading, the triangle is the strongest basic geometric shape known to man, which is why it is used to support a roof in a domestic building for example. It is this very strength of the triangle which is significant in a reading. It infers that the sitter has a strong character, as in moral strength rather than physical strength. Whatever life throws at this particular sitter, they can handle it.

70 The Seven of Wands / Rods

Battle

Symbolises conflict or struggle.

Within a reading, a battle scene represents that the sitter is experiencing some kind of struggle in their life. This could be an emotional struggle, or possibly a struggle with a legal procedure.

Door (Portal)

Symbolises the opening to a new path in life.

Within a reading, any door of any shape, size or colour represents that the sitter is about to open that door and start out on a new path in life. Of course, this door may well have just opened for the sitter and they have already begun their journey.

Mountains

Symbolises challenges.

Within a reading, mountains usually appear in the background of the card. For the sitter, this suggests that they are facing seemingly insurmountable challenges, but that the sitter is trying to ignore them, pushing them to the back of their mind. If mountains appear in the majority of the spread, this indicates that the time has come for the sitter to face those challenges and to deal with them.

Rock

Symbolises dependability.

Within a reading, the appearance of a rock (or rocks) suggests that the sitter is one of life's more dependable souls. Their passion and determination is apparent in everything that they do. It shows that they have the personal strength to overcome the situations that life throws at them. The old sayings 'as solid as a rock' and 'he/she is my rock' definitely apply to this sitter.

Snow (Snowflakes)

Symbolises a fresh start.

Within a reading, snow can have two interpretations. In the first instance, the sitter might be feeling that some important information is being kept from them. They might feel that they are getting the 'cold shoulder' or that they are being 'kept out in the cold' because something is being withheld. On the other hand, a blanket of snow can represent a fresh start, a whole new beginning, as the blanket of snow gives promise of the springtime to come.

Stairway

Symbolises a new path or goal.

Within a reading, a stairway can often suggest that the sitter is about to start on a whole new path in life. This could simply be the first tentative step on the ladder to a new career, or the beginning of a new goal that the sitter has set for themselves. It can also represent that the sitter has started to take their own spirituality to another level. For example, they might be starting to become aware of their own psychic abilities and that they have started to explore the possibilities.

71 The Eight of Wands / Rods

Centaur

Symbolises unity of the mind and body.

Within a reading, the appearance of a centaur infers that the sitter might be in need of trying to strike a balance between their 'spiritual' and 'animal' sides. In other words, it is possible that they are knowingly doing something wrong and it is going against the grain.

Clouds

Symbolises transition.

Within a reading, clouds have different meanings depending on what colour they are. In the suit of Swords, most of the clouds are dark and fast moving, representing that the sitter is probably going through a troublesome (or stormy) period in their life. However, dark clouds like these can also represent confusion, or clouded judgement.

Mountains

Symbolises challenges.

Within a reading, mountains usually appear in the background of the card. For the sitter, this suggests that they are facing seemingly insurmountable challenges, but that the sitter is trying to ignore them, pushing them to the back of their mind. If mountains appear in the majority of the spread, this indicates that the time has come for the sitter to face those challenges and to deal with them.

Ribbons

Symbolises fragility.

Within a reading, ribbons should never be ignored, as they bring to our attention just how fragile the bonds that bind us really are. The sitter should take a good look at the relationships that they have with those who are closest to them. Are they treating their loved ones, their friends or colleagues with the respect that they deserve? If not, they could end up forcing then away.

River

Symbolises obstacles.

Within a reading, the appearance of a river can be interpreted in two different ways. For the sitter, a river can represent an obstacle that they have to get across, as it is blocking their path or progress. On the other hand, it could be advising the sitter to stop struggling with whatever problem that they are facing or dealing with. It is time for them to 'go with the flow' and let the problem resolve itself.

Snow (Snowflakes)

Symbolises a fresh start.

Within a reading, snow can have two interpretations. In the first instance, the sitter might be feeling that some important information is being kept from them. They might feel that they are getting the 'cold shoulder' or that they are being 'kept out in the cold' because something is being withheld. On the other hand, a blanket of snow can represent a fresh start, a whole new beginning, as the blanket of snow gives promise of the springtime to come.

Trees

Symbolises growth.

Within a reading, trees appear in many of the Tarot Cards, but significantly, they usually appear in the background. If trees appear in a lot of the cards within a spread, then this indicates that the sitter has plans for a new venture, path or phase in their life. However, at the moment, these plans are at the back of the sitter's mind. These plans are something that the sitter is considering putting into action in the near future, as they are still working on them, costing them out or carrying out research.

72 The Nine of Wands / Rods

Arm Band

Symbolises belonging.

Within a reading, an armband represents the need of the sitter to belong to something. This might be a group or organisation that the sitter feels attracted to.

(An armband can be a piece of material, a piece of jewellery or even a tattoo.)

Gauntlets (Gloves)

Symbolises a challenge.

Within a reading, the appearance of a gauntlet represents that the sitter is facing some kind of challenge in their life, as in 'throwing down the gauntlet'. This could be a challenge that they face, or a challenge that they have made.

Hills

Symbolises obstacles.

Within a reading, the appearance of hills in the spread suggests that the sitter is facing obstacles in their life that they need to overcome. However daunting or impossible these hurdles might appear to be for the sitter, they need to remove these obstacles in their life in order to move on.

Moon

Symbolises cycles.

Within a reading, the appearance of the moon in a spread indicates that the sitter is moving from one phase of their life to another. Whatever transition is taking place in the sitter's life, it is for the sitter's overall good and/or wellbeing. The moon can also indicate that the sitter is quite a spiritual person, who might very well be starting to realise that they have psychic abilities themselves.

Red Sky

Symbolises trouble ahead.

Within a reading, the red sky is not telling the sitter that tomorrow will be a nice day as the old saying goes. It appears in the spread as a warning of trouble ahead. The sitter may not know what this warning refers to, but now is the time for the sitter to anticipate the probable problem, or problems that are coming their way and to prepare for it.

Sunset

Symbolises an ending.

Within a reading, the image of a sunset infers that some aspect of the sitter's life is winding down or coming to an end. This could be a period of intense work, a difficult phase, a troubling time or maybe just the end of a project that has taken longer to complete than anticipated. Whatever it is that is coming to an end, it is now time for the sitter to relax, as the worst is now over.

73 The Ten of Wands / Rods

Castle

Symbolises goals and achievements.

Within a reading, a castle represents the sitter's long and difficult journey to achieve their goal in life. This might be a long university degree course, or a long battle against illness. Whatever the sitter's goal is, they are well on their way to achieving it. On a simpler note, a castle can represent security or sanctuary.

Mountains

Symbolises challenges.

Within a reading, mountains usually appear in the background of the card. For the sitter, this suggests that they are facing seemingly insurmountable challenges, but that the sitter is trying to ignore them, pushing them to the back of their mind. If mountains appear in the majority of the spread, this indicates that the time has come for the sitter to face those challenges and to deal with them.

Path (Road)

Symbolises life choices.

Within a reading, a path or a road refers to the fact that the sitter is facing a new path in life. The sitter might be about to set out on that new path, or may already have taken their first few steps on it. Either way, this path represents a whole new and potentially exciting future for the sitter. If they are having any doubts about this new path, they shouldn't worry, as it will be the right choice for them.

Ploughed Fields

Symbolises care and planning.

Within a reading, ploughed fields remind the sitter that 'we reap what we sew'. The sitter must keep in mind that whatever they do today will ultimately affect their future plans and outcomes. The sitter will benefit from a bit of careful thought and planning before they start any new venture. It would be helpful if the sitter remembers that ploughed fields can also represent time. Just as it takes time for crops to grow, so it takes time for our plans to come to fruition, so the sitter must try and understand that patience will be required.

Trees

Symbolises growth.

Within a reading, trees appear in many of the Tarot Cards, but significantly, they usually appear in the background. If trees appear in a lot of the cards within a spread, then this indicates that the sitter has plans for a new venture, path or phase in their life. However, at the moment, these plans are at the back of the sitter's mind. These plans are something that the sitter is considering putting into action in the near future, as they are still working on them, costing them out or carrying out research.

Triangle

Symbolises strength.

Within a reading, the triangle is the strongest basic geometric shape known to man, which is why it is used to support a roof in a domestic building for example. It is this very strength of the triangle which is significant in a reading. It infers that the sitter has a strong character, as in moral strength rather than physical strength. Whatever life throws at this particular sitter, they can handle it.

74 The Page of Wands / Rods

Dragon

Symbolises wisdom, strength and courage.

Within a reading, the appearance of a dragon in the spread represents that the sitter needs to rise over their present circumstances in order to see things more clearly. Whatever their currant problem is, they need moral strength and personal courage to overcome it.

Lizard

Symbolises renewal and rebirth.

Within a reading, the appearance of a lizard infers that the sitter is about to enter a phase of clear vision and enlightenment in their life. This is most probably connected to the sitter's realisation that a new opportunity is presenting itself to them. This new opportunity will offer the sitter a whole new start.

Mountains

Symbolises challenges.

Within a reading, mountains usually appear in the background of the card. For the sitter, this suggests that they are facing seemingly insurmountable challenges, but that the sitter is trying to ignore them, pushing them to the back of their mind. If mountains appear in the majority of the spread, this indicates that the time has come for the sitter to face those challenges and to deal with them.

Ruff (Collar)

Symbolises stiffness of attitude.

Within a reading, the ruff was a stiffly starched decorative collar worn by the Elizabethans who believed that it displayed their mastery over their bodily sensations. For the present day sitter however, the meaning is a little less pompous. It can simply represent the fact that the sitter is being a little 'stiff-necked' about something. The time has come for the sitter to relax a bit, let go and enjoy life more.

Sea (Ocean)

Symbolises an unsettled time.

Within a reading, the appearance of the sea is designed to make us think about our life. The sitter should consider the vastness and the strength of the sea. It can be calm, but it can suddenly turn violent and unleash its power. For the sitter this can indicate that their life has recently been full of ups and downs, as situations ebb and flow through their recent daily routine. They probably feel as if they have recently been washed about from pillar to post. Calm will return, but they will have to be patient and ride out the storm.

Sun

Symbolises life and rebirth.

Within a reading, just as the sun rises every morning, so a new day begins for the sitter. The position of the sun in a Tarot card is also significant. A rising sun promises new beginnings, while a setting sun infers that something is coming to an end. A full mid-day sun indicates energy, strength and success in creative endeavours.

Tassels

Symbolises achievement.

Within a reading, as tassels have always been associated with power, position and prestige, they are a good sign for the sitter. They foretell the achievement of desires or goals and as such, are a sign of success. They can also represent victory, or success over whatever hardships that the sitter is currently facing at the moment. If they stay resolute, they will overcome those hardships and come through it all successfully.

Triangle

Symbolises strength.

Within a reading, the triangle is the strongest basic geometric shape known to man, which is why it is used to support a roof in a domestic building for example. It is this very strength of the triangle which is significant in a reading. It infers that the sitter has a strong character, as in moral strength rather than physical strength. Whatever life throws at this particular sitter, they can handle it.

75 The Knight of Wands / Rods

Armour

Symbolises protection and strength.

Within a reading, the appearance of armour suggests that the sitter is feeling vulnerable in some way and that they feel the need to protect themselves from their perceived threat.

Dragon

Symbolises wisdom, strength and courage.

Within a reading, the appearance of a dragon in the spread represents that the sitter needs to rise over their present circumstances in order to see things more clearly. Whatever their currant problem is, they need moral strength and personal courage to overcome it.

Feathers

Symbolises spiritual evolution.

Within a reading, a feather (or feathers) represents that the sitter is becoming aware of their spiritual side and that they are probably keen to advance that interest. Within the spiritual movement, feathers are universally recognised as a sign from Spirit, or a loved one that has passed.

Fire (Flames)

Symbolises transformation.

Within a reading, fire or flames represents that the sitter is going through some kind of transition in their life. They can also represent that the sitter might need to make some kind of change, alteration or modification to their lifestyle.

Helmet

Symbolises protection.

Within a reading, a helmet can suggest that the sitter is feeling vulnerable in some way and is looking for a way to protect themselves from the cause. Usually a helmet has a plume or crest on top of it for identification. This could suggest that the sitter is searching for acceptance in some way.

Horns

Symbolises physical prowess.

Within a reading, the appearance of horns indicates that the sitter is experiencing (or is in need of) fighting spirit in order to overcome a challenge that they are currently facing. It can also infer that the sitter has to take this challenge head on (by the horns), as there is really no other way of dealing with it.

Horse

Symbolises strength and freedom.

Within a reading, a horse refers to the sitter's personal drive and a desire to free themselves from the current path that they are following. The sitter has the strength and stamina to easily achieve this goal, but they have to believe in themselves. Horses are also regarded as a deep spiritual sign, which might hint at the sitter's need for some spiritual guidance. Maybe the sitter needs to free themselves from old beliefs.

Lizard

Symbolises renewal and rebirth.

Within a reading, the appearance of a lizard infers that the sitter is about to enter a phase of clear vision and enlightenment in their life. This is most probably connected to the sitter's realisation that a new opportunity is presenting itself to them. This new opportunity will offer the sitter a whole new start.

Mountains

Symbolises challenges.

Within a reading, mountains usually appear in the background of the card. For the sitter, this suggests that they are facing seemingly insurmountable challenges, but that the sitter is trying to ignore them, pushing them to the back of their mind. If mountains appear in the majority of the spread, this indicates that the time has come for the sitter to face those challenges and to deal with them.

Red Sky

Symbolises trouble ahead.

Within a reading, the red sky is not telling the sitter that tomorrow will be a nice day as the old saying goes. It appears in the spread as a warning of trouble ahead. The sitter may not know what this warning refers to, but now is the time for the sitter to anticipate the probable problem, or problems that are coming their way and to prepare for it.

Trees

Symbolises growth.

Within a reading, trees appear in many of the Tarot Cards, but significantly, they usually appear in the background. If trees appear in a lot of the cards within a spread, then this indicates that the sitter has plans for a new venture, path or phase in their life. However, at the moment, these plans are at the back of the sitter's mind. These plans are something that the sitter is considering putting into action in the near future, as they are still working on them, costing them out or carrying out research.

76 The Queen of Wands / Rods

Braids

Symbolises spiritual strength and health.

Within a reading, the appearance of braided hair (three strands of hair woven together) represents the sitter's mind, body and spirit being strengthened by a new influence in their life.

Cat

Symbolises spiritual ability.

Within a reading, the appearance of a cat in the spread denotes the sitter's quest for spiritual enlightenment. Not necessarily in a religious sense (although it could be), but possibly just seeking a path in life that can liberate them and make them feel free. In this case, a cat would indicate that the sitter is burdened with too many responsibilities.

Crown

Symbolises authority and power.

Within a reading, the appearance of a crown can signify many things. It could suggest that the sitter needs authority in their life. Possibly that the sitter desires recognition for their achievements. Or even that the sitter desires more control of their life, which might feel a little out of control to them at the moment.

Lion

Symbolises courage and strength.

Within a reading, a lion can indicate that the sitter has the necessary personal courage and emotional strength required to overcome the difficulties that they are facing right now. Just as the lion is fearless, it is time for the sitter to conquer his or her own fears. Fear can hold us back, so conquering your fears will is the key to the sitter achieving the success that they desire.

Mountains

Symbolises challenges.

Within a reading, mountains usually appear in the background of the card. For the sitter, this suggests that they are facing seemingly insurmountable challenges, but that the sitter is trying to ignore them, pushing them to the back of their mind. If mountains appear in the majority of the spread, this indicates that the time has come for the sitter to face those challenges and to deal with them.

Sunflower

Symbolises positivity.

Within a reading, because sunflowers are such 'happy' flowers, they brighten up the lives of all who look at them. For the sitter however, it can imply that they are feeling a little down, in the doldrums so to speak. The sunflower is urging the sitter to stop looking at the dark side of their situation, as focusing on what is wrong in their life will only depress them more. They should start looking at the lighter side of life, as concentrating on the good or happy things in life will lift their mood.

Throne

Symbolises stability.

Within a reading, as a throne is a seat of authority, this represents a position of responsibility for the sitter. Some aspect of the sitter's life is completely under their control. This could be a position at work, as in a managerial post. Possibly at home where the sitter has sole responsibility for raising a child or caring for someone for example. Whichever aspect of the sitter's life the throne refers to, it is running smoothly, but only because of the sitter's determination and steady hand.

Veil

Symbolises mysticism.

Within a reading, a veil can represent two sides of the same coin. On the one hand, a veil can indicate that the sitter is hiding behind a façade, not allowing the world to see the real person inside. On the other hand, a veil can represent that the sitter possesses hidden knowledge, usually of a spiritual or psychic nature. Either way, the sitter sits behind a veil of mysticism and is usually an old soul with life experiences beyond their years.

77 The King of Wands / Rods

Altar

Symbolises a sacred place.

Within a reading, an altar implies that the sitter is in need of some personal space within their busy life. They need this personal space in order to have some time to themselves, maybe to pursue their interest in a hobby, or more importantly, to develop their individual spirituality.

Crown

Symbolises authority and power.

Within a reading, the appearance of a crown can signify many things. It could suggest that the sitter needs authority in their life. Possibly that the sitter desires recognition for their achievements. Or even that the sitter desires more control of their life, which might feel a little out of control to them at the moment.

Dragon

Symbolises wisdom, strength and courage.

Within a reading, the appearance of a dragon in the spread represents that the sitter needs to rise over their present circumstances in order to see things more clearly. Whatever their currant problem is, they need moral strength and personal courage to overcome it.

Fire (Flames)

Symbolises transformation.

Within a reading, fire or flames represents that the sitter is going through some kind of transition in their life. They can also represent that the sitter might need to make some kind of change, alteration or modification to their lifestyle.

Horns

Symbolises physical prowess.

Within a reading, the appearance of horns indicates that the sitter is experiencing (or is in need of) fighting spirit in order to overcome a challenge that they are currently facing. It can also infer that the sitter has to take this challenge head on (by the horns), as there is really no other way of dealing with it.

Lion

Symbolises courage and strength.

Within a reading, a lion can indicate that the sitter has the necessary personal courage and emotional strength required to overcome the difficulties that they are facing right now. Just as the lion is fearless, it is time for the sitter to conquer his or her own fears. Fear can hold us back, so conquering your fears will is the key to the sitter achieving the success that they desire.

Lizard

Symbolises renewal and rebirth.

Within a reading, the appearance of a lizard infers that the sitter is about to enter a phase of clear vision and enlightenment in their life. This is most probably connected to the sitter's realisation that a new opportunity is presenting itself to them. This new opportunity will offer the sitter a whole new start.

Mountains

Symbolises challenges.

Within a reading, mountains usually appear in the background of the card. For the sitter, this suggests that they are facing seemingly insurmountable challenges, but that the sitter is trying to ignore them, pushing them to the back of their mind. If mountains appear in the majority of the spread, this indicates that the time has come for the sitter to face those challenges and to deal with them.

Pillar

Symbolises stability.

Within a reading, a pillar or pillars, represent strength, stability and balance. A single pillar can suggest that the sitter is the one who is supporting those around them, as in 'a pillar of strength'. When two pillars appear, usually at each side of the card, this could indicate that the sitter should consider their problems in a more diplomatic, or balanced way. Rather than left or right or black and white, the sitter should try to consider a more central view. In other words, the sitter should adopt a new perspective, a middle-of-the-road approach when tackling their problems.

Throne

Symbolises stability.

Within a reading, as a throne is a seat of authority, this represents a position of responsibility for the sitter. Some aspect of the sitter's life is completely under their control. This could be a position at work, as in a managerial post. Possibly at home where the sitter has sole responsibility for raising a child or caring for someone for example. Whichever aspect of the sitter's life the throne refers to, it is running smoothly, but only because of the sitter's determination and steady hand.

Index

Manufactured by Amazon.ca
Bolton, ON